PHOTODELUXE

in eas

NICK VANDOME

COMPUTER STEP

In easy steps is an imprint of Computer Step
Southfield Road . Southam
Warwickshire CV47 OFB . England

http://www.ineasysteps.com

Notice of Liability

Every effort has been made to ensure that this book contains accurate and current information. However, Computer Step and the author shall not be liable for any loss or damage suffered by readers as a result of any information contained herein.

Trademarks

PhotoDeluxe is a trademark of Adobe Systems Incorporated. All other trademarks are acknowledged as belonging to their respective companies.

Printed and bound in the United Kingdom

ISBN 1-84078-083-5

Contents

Introducing PhotoDeluxe

PhotoDeluxe is a powerful, all-purpose image editing program that can be used to enhance images, create projects such as cards and calendars and also share images over the Internet. This chapter shows how to obtain and install the program, details the work area, menus and toolbars and covers the basics of image file formats and memory issues.

Covers

Chapter One

Overview

For a complete overview of PhotoDeluxe and the other Adobe products, which include desktop publishing, image editing and Web design software, go to their Website at www.adobe.com

The colour editing, touch-up techniques and special effects are almost identical between the different versions of PhotoDeluxe. Version 4.0 has greater compatibility with posting images on the Web, but the other versions are equally capable of manipulating images and creating projects.

With the world of photography enthusiastically embracing the digital era, in the form of digital cameras that can cost thousands of pounds to ones that are under £100, it is no surprise that there has been a growth industry in software designed to edit and manipulate these images. As with the cameras, these range from professional programs, such as Adobe Photoshop, to the consumer level ones, including PhotoDeluxe. Although PhotoDeluxe can be bought for under £50, it is nevertheless an extremely versatile and effective program. Its maker, Adobe, is a world leader in image editing software and this experience and expertise are packed into PhotoDeluxe.

In addition to containing powerful editing functions for adjusting the colour of images and eliminating elements such as wrinkles and red-eye, PhotoDeluxe also has facilities for incorporating images into special projects such as cards, calendars or on-screen slide shows. The latest release of the program (version 4.0) also comes with enhanced options for sharing images, either by email or over the Web. This can be used to place your images within a private community on the Web. Your images can then be viewed by anyone you invite to join your online community. The sharing facilities also enable you to create items such as online puzzles and postcards. There is also a business version, which is geared towards creating workplace documents and presentations. This has similar functions for editing images and adding them into a variety of publications. However, it does not have the same capabilities for sharing images.

Although version 4.0 of PhotoDeluxe is only for Windows, there is also a version 2.0 for the Mac. This has almost identical editing functions and special effects to version 4.0 for Windows, but it does not have as powerful sharing facilities.

Obtaining PhotoDeluxe

There are three main ways of obtaining PhotoDeluxe:

- From a software retailer. Most computer shops that sell software will sell PhotoDeluxe or be able to order it for you. The cost should be approximately £45

- From the Adobe Website. The program can be downloaded from here directly onto your computer. On the home page, select the Products button and then select PhotoDeluxe from the list that appears. You will have to use a credit card to pay for the program, after which it can be downloaded by following the on-screen instructions. If you are buying the program in the UK, go to the corresponding Website at www.adobe.co.uk

If you download PhotoDeluxe from the Adobe Website, this gives you the added advantage of being able to register the software at the same time. This will entitle you to product support and Adobe will also inform you of any upgrades when they are published.

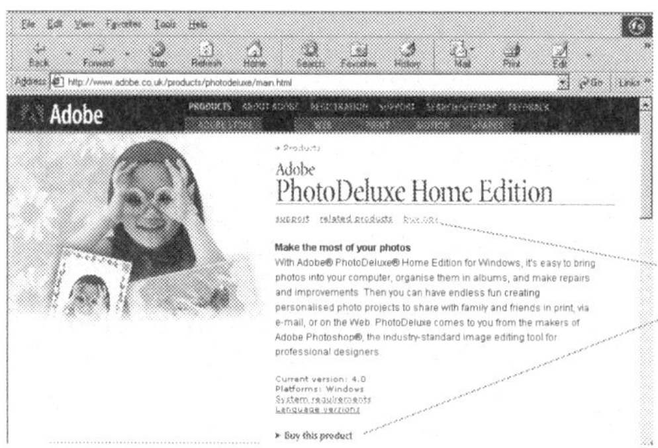

Go to the PhotoDeluxe page on the Adobe Website and click on either of these buttons to download the program

Do not be put off by a particular digital imaging device, just because you do not like the software that comes bundled with it. A camera or a scanner will probably be more expensive than an image editing program and so it is best to buy the device that you want and then, if necessary, buy the software, such as PhotoDeluxe, separately.

- With digital imaging devices. One of the most popular ways of getting PhotoDeluxe into the marketplace is to bundle it with digital cameras and scanners. This then gives the user the means to not only capture images, but to edit them as well. If you are buying one of these devices, check to see what software is provided with it. If you do not like what is being offered, try negotiating for something better, such as PhotoDeluxe

Installing

System requirements

PhotoDeluxe can be installed either from a CD-ROM or directly onto your hard drive from the Adobe Website. Both methods then take you through the installation process, at which point you can specify which components you want to install.

When installing PhotoDeluxe you can either choose the full installation or the custom one. The full one includes all of the elements on the CD-ROM or the download site and the custom one allows you to choose which components you want to install. If you decide not to install a certain element, you can always go back and do so at a later date. See the next page for the elements that come with PhotoDeluxe.

To install PhotoDeluxe 4.0 with Windows:

- Pentium II 233 MHz processor or equivalent
- Windows 95, Windows 98 or Windows NT 4.0
- 32 Mb of RAM (64 Mb for Windows NT)
- 100 Mb of hard disk space
- Colour monitor with 800 x 600 resolution
- CD-ROM drive
- An Internet connection for the Web sharing facilities

Image editing is very memory hungry and so the more RAM and hard disk space that you have available, the better.

For running PhotoDeluxe 2.0 on a Mac:

- 68040 or Power Macintosh processor
- Apple System OS 7.2 or later
- 16 Mb of available RAM
- 70 Mb of available hard disk space
- Colour monitor with support for 256 colours
- CD-ROM drive

Elements of PhotoDeluxe

When you install PhotoDeluxe 4.0 or download it from the Adobe Website the following elements are included:

- PhotoDeluxe. This is the main element and consists of the software for image editing and manipulation

The ActiveShare software links into a site on the Web which is dedicated to sharing digital images. It allows users to set up their own private communities (called eCircles) to which family and friends can be invited to view images and also add their own. The ActiveShare Website is at:

www.activeshare.com

This is looked at in greater detail in Chapter Eleven.

- ActiveShare. This is a program that can also be used as an image editing tool, but its main function is for sharing images over the Web

ActiveShare can be used for image editing and sharing images on the Web

PDF files can be used to preserve the original formatting of a document such as a newsletter or a brochure. Because of this it is a popular format for displaying documents on the Web. In order to be able to view them you need Adobe Acrobat reader, which is free and well worth having.

- Over 1,000 templates and clip art images that can be used for creative projects
- PhotoParade. This can be used for creating on-screen displays and slide shows
- Adobe Acrobat Reader 4.0. This is a program that can be used to view Portable Document Format (PDF) files

Image issues

Before getting started with PhotoDeluxe, it is a good idea to have a general understanding of digital images and how they work.

Pixels

Digital images that are captured with a digital camera or a scanner are made up of pixels. These are tiny dots of colour and they are the building blocks upon which these images are built. If you look very closely at a digital image you will be able to see the individual pixels. However, when you view it from a few feet away, all of the pixels should merge together to give a smooth image. In general, the more pixels in an image then the higher the quality. Depending on the quality of the device being used, the pixels in some images can contain a greater variety of colour information than in those captured with inferior equipment. If an image is of poor quality then it may appear pixelated i.e. you will be able to see the individual pixels and the overall appearance of the image will be ragged rather than smooth.

Resolution

Resolution can be one of the more complicated aspects of digital images, because it refers to so many different things. In general, it is all about the number of pixels relating to an image. The main areas of resolution that concern digital imaging are:

The higher the resolution of an image, then the larger the file size. This could have an impact when you are editing an image or sharing it on the Web.

- Camera resolution. This is the number of pixels that a camera is capable of capturing for an image. The higher the number, then the better the quality will be. With the price of digital cameras falling all the time, it is worth looking for one that can capture as many pixels as possible. Try for a minimum of 1200 x 800 pixels, which is over 1 million in total. This accounts for the actual size of the image — the size at which it is displayed or printed depends on the settings chosen in PhotoDeluxe

- Image resolution. This is the size at which an image is printed at or displayed on the Web. This can be set within PhotoDeluxe and it is measured in pixels per inch (ppi). So if an image's actual size was 1200 pixels by 900 pixels and the image resolution was set to 300 ppi, then the image would be printed or displayed at 4 inches by 3 inches (1200 divided by 300 = 4, and 900 divided by 300 = 3). In order to make an image larger, the image resolution would have to be decreased. If it were set at 100 ppi then the above image would be displayed at 12 inches by 9 inches. However, this would impair the quality of the image as each pixel would have to be stretched to cover the extra area. Changing the image resolution does not change the physical size of an image i.e. the actual number of pixels which it contains. An image that is made up of 1 million pixels, will still have that number if it were displayed at 100 ppi or 300 ppi. Only the size at which it were printed or displayed on the Web would be altered

If you are using images for sharing on the Web then the maximum image resolution can be set to between 72–96 ppi. This is because this is the highest number that most computer monitors can display, so anything higher would just be wasted.

Dots per inch and pixels per inch are not the same thing, although they are frequently treated as being interchangeable. Pixels per inch refer to the size of an image and dots per inch refer to the quality of a printed image.

- Print resolution. To confuse the issue further, printers also have a resolution setting which is measured in dots per inch (dpi). This is the number of dots of colour that will be used to cover each inch of the image, regardless of the number of pixels that make up that inch. If there were ten pixels in an inch then the printer would still use the same number of dots as if there were 1000 pixels. The standard dpi output for colour inkjet printers is 300, although some go up to 1440. If you are going to be printing a lot of images from PhotoDeluxe, then go for a printer with as high a dpi as possible — the difference between a 300 dpi and a 1440 dpi can be remarkable

Resizing

Digital images can be resized in PhotoDeluxe for the purpose of making them larger, smaller or changing the file size. An image can be resized by changing the image resolution or by changing the output size of the image, or both. There are a number of ways to access the Photo Size dialog box and these will be dealt with as they occur through the book. However, even at this point it is useful to understand the general idea behind image resizing:

When capturing images, some digital cameras and scanners can increase the overall number of pixels that are captured through the use of a technique called interpolation. This is in effect just some fancy digital guess work, where the device adds pixels by trying to match them to the existing ones in an image. While this can produce an image with more pixels it is not the best way to achieve this and can result in inferior quality.

1. Select Size>Photo Size from the Advanced Menu bar

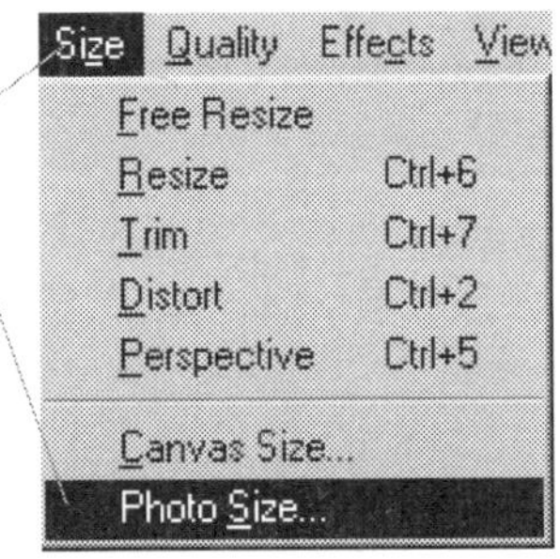

To access the Advanced Menu bar, select the Advanced Menu button at the bottom of the Open Photo area.

2. To change the image resolution, enter new values here. The original settings are displayed at the top while the new settings are displayed at the bottom. Note how the file size stays the same but the display size (width and height) changes. Make sure the two boxes at the bottom are checked on. If the width and height boxes are altered, then the resolution changes automatically

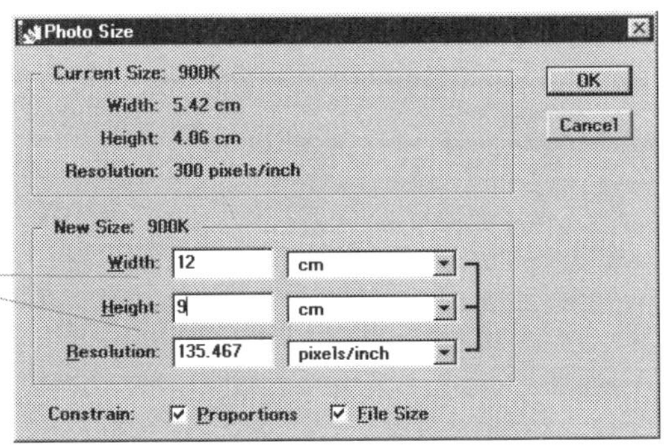

See the facing page for details about the PhotoDeluxe interface and accessing menus and toolbars.

Opening up

Once PhotoDeluxe has been installed it can be opened in two ways:

- Double-click the PhotoDeluxe icon on the desktop
- Select Start>Programs>Adobe>PhotoDeluxe>PhotoDeluxe in Windows (Apple Menu>Macintosh HD>Adobe PhotoDeluxe on a Mac)

If the PhotoDeluxe icon does not appear on the desktop in Windows, a shortcut to the program can be placed there by locating the program file in Windows Explorer. Right-click on it and drag the icon onto the desktop and then release. Select Create Shortcut Here and the PhotoDeluxe icon will be included on the desktop. If you double-click on it, the program will launch.

When the program first opens, the following screen appears:

The Menu bar

The toolbars. Various options are available within each one

The Advanced Menu button. Click here to access a wider choice of menus

The workspace. This is where images appear when they are opened in PhotoDeluxe

Shortcuts toolbar

The Open Photo area above the Advanced Menu button is used to display thumbnails of all of the images that you currently have open. This can be a useful way to keep track of what you are working on.

The Shortcut toolbar can be used to move quickly to commonly used items within PhotoDeluxe. To show and hide this toolbar, click on the PhotoDeluxe icon at the bottom right of the screen.

Opening images

The first step in getting started with PhotoDeluxe is to open an image:

All of the commands on the toolbars can also be accessed from the Menu bar, but at this stage it is probably easier to select them via the toolbar buttons.

1 Select the Get & Fix Photo button

2 Select the Get Photo button. (A range of options for obtaining an image are dealt with in more detail in Chapter Two)

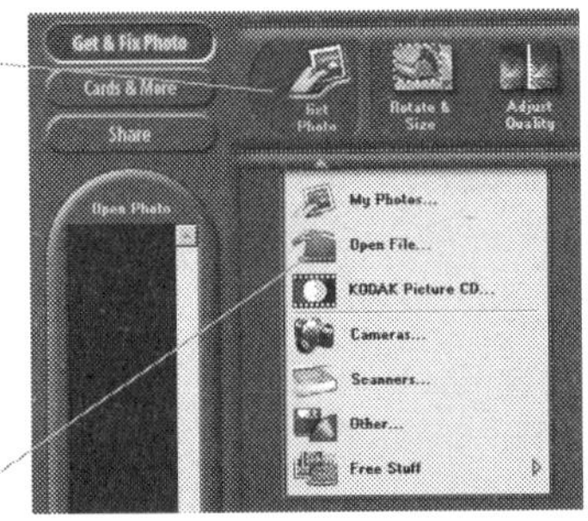

Images can be placed onto a hard drive using a digital camera, a scanner or a form of removable storage such as a floppy disc. Images can also be downloaded from the Web and saved to your hard disk. To do this, right-click (Ctrl+click on a Mac) on an image that you want to save and select Save Picture As and save it to the relevant folder on your computer.

3 Select Open File and select an image from your hard drive. Select Open

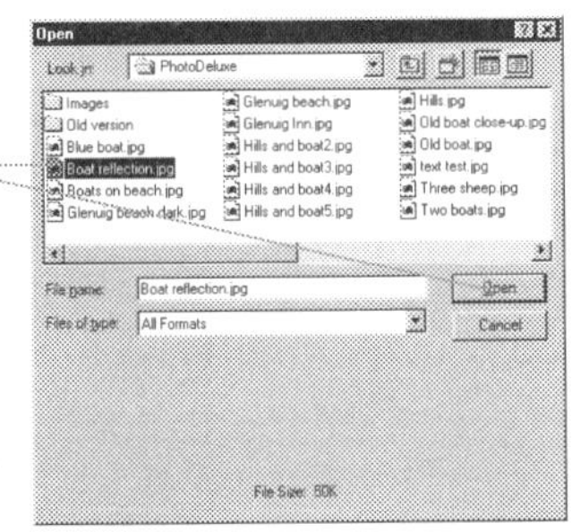

4 The image will be displayed in the work area

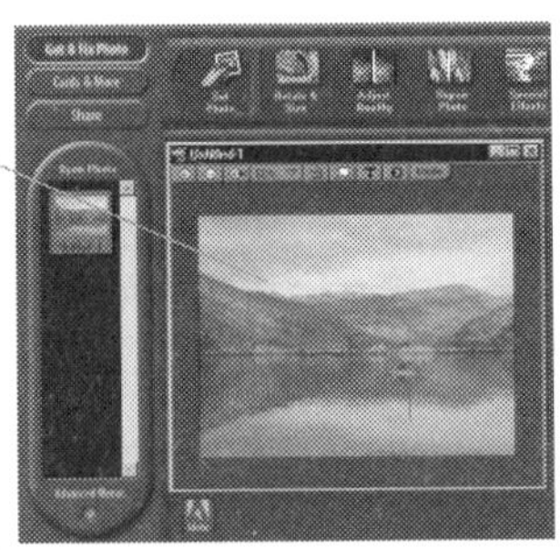

Viewing images

When you are working with images you will want to perform different tasks at various points throughout the editing process. This could include zooming in to a particular part of the image to remove a blemish, or positioning an element such as a block of text.

Zooming in and out

PhotoDeluxe employs several methods by which you can alter how you view an image.

In order to use the greatest screen area for working on an image, make sure the work area is maximised, by clicking on the small icon with a square inside it (the button with a square in the top left-hand corner on a Mac) at the top right-hand corner of the screen.

3 Click here to zoom in on a specific area. A magnifying glass icon will appear – click and drag it over the area you want to enlarge (or hold down Alt to decrease)

1 Click here to increase the overall magnification

2 Click here to decrease the overall magnification

Working closely with images on a computer monitor can be very tiring on the eyes, so make sure you take regular breaks.

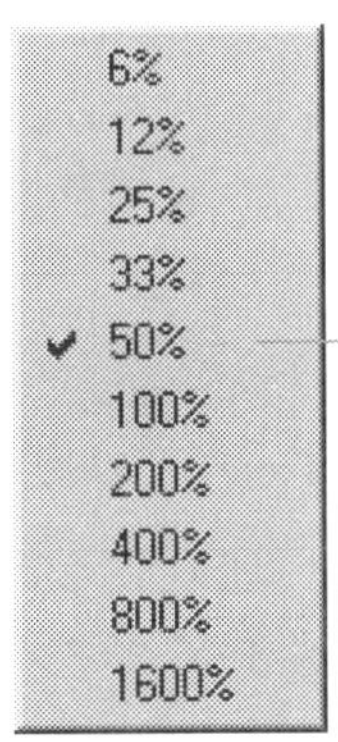

4 Click here to access a drop down menu which can be used to set a specific viewing size

Using rulers

PhotoDeluxe has a function for displaying rulers above and to the side of an image, which can be useful for positioning items and also seeing the actual size of an image, regardless of the size at which it is being viewed. To use the rulers:

1. Select the Advanced Menu button

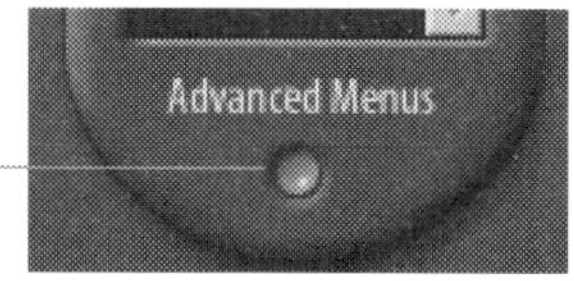

2. Select View>Show Rulers from the Advanced Menu

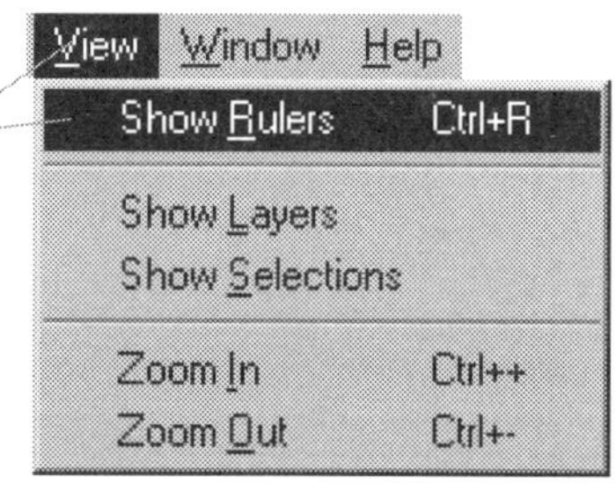

It is possible to change the zero point of the rulers. To do this, click and hold on the intersecting lines in the top left-hand corner of the rulers. Then drag across the image until you reach the point where you want the new zero point. To reset the zero point, double-click in the top left-hand corner of the rulers.

3. The rulers appear above and to the left of the open image

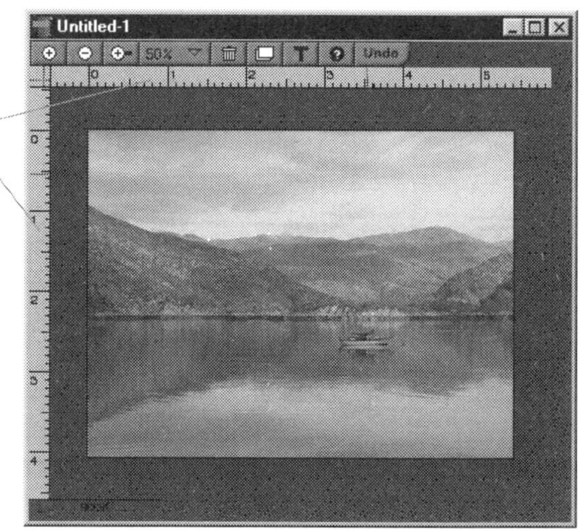

It is also possible to set preferences for the way that the rulers are displayed:

There are a variety of options for default settings and they will be dealt with at the relevant points at which they occur.

1 Select File>Preferences> Units from the Menu bar

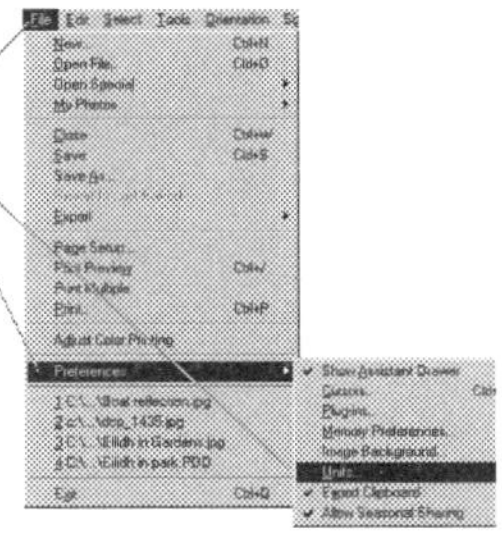

2 Click here to set the unit of measurement that you want the rulers to be displayed in (the other settings can be left at their default values)

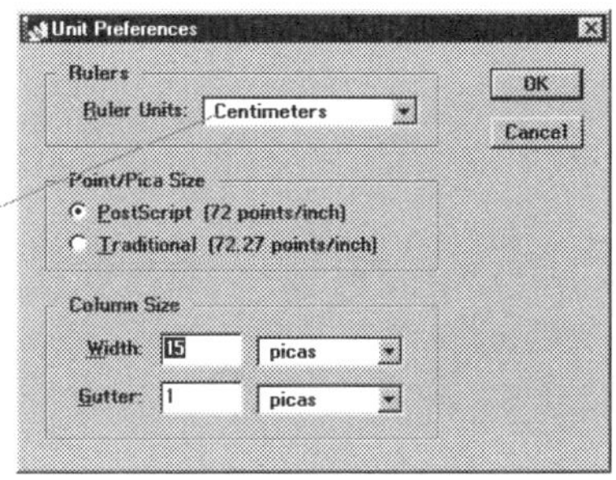

The Wastebasket can be used to remove elements that have been added to an image (such as a text block) rather than the actual image itself.

Image toolbar options

In addition to the options for setting the magnification level, the other options on the toolbar that appears above an open image in the work area are:

The Wastebasket

PhotoDeluxe Help

The stacking order of elements within the image

The Text tool

Undo button

The Undo button can only be used for the immediately previous action — it cannot undo a string of actions.

Menus

There are three standard PhotoDeluxe menus. The Advanced Menus contain a much wider range of choice which will be looked at as their functions occur throughout the book. However, these are usually also covered by the functions contained within the toolbars.

File menu

The File menu contains the following commands:

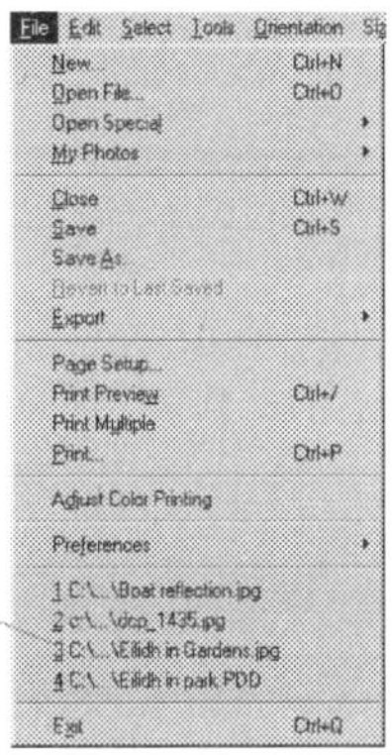

The area at the bottom of the File menu displays the most recently opened images. This can be a useful shortcut for opening files that you want to work on again.

You can create new albums in which to store your images by selecting My Photos>Create New Album. The My Photos function also displays albums that have been created in ActiveShare. Images can be added to these albums from PhotoDeluxe. For more information on ActiveShare, see Chapter Eleven.

- New. This opens a new, blank file with no image in it
- Open File. This opens an image from a chosen location
- Open Special. This enables you to open an image in a specified image format
- My Photos. This enables you to open images that have been organised into specific collections
- Close. This closes the active image file
- Save. This saves the active image file
- Save As. This can be used to save an image file under another name i.e. make a copy of it

- Revert to Last Saved. This can be used to go back to the last saved version of an image. This is useful if you have made a lot of editing changes that you do not want to keep

Use Export if you want to save an image into a specific file format, such as a JPEG. If you just select Save, then PhotoDeluxe will use its own proprietary file format, which has either a ".pdd" or a "*.pbd" file extension. For more on file formats, see page 25.*

- Export. This can be used to save images into a different file format
- Page Setup. This contains settings for how images are printed
- Print Preview. This shows how the printed image will appear
- Print Multiple. This can be used to print several copies of the same image on a page
- Print. This prints the current active image file

Use Print Preview to make sure that the current size of your image will fit onto the size of paper that you are printing on.

- Adjust Colour Printing. This can be used to alter the way the printed image appears
- Preferences. This controls various elements of the program
- Exit. This closes PhotoDeluxe

Help menu

The Help menu contains an index of help topics and also a search facility for specific topics.

Edit menu

The Edit menu contains the following commands:

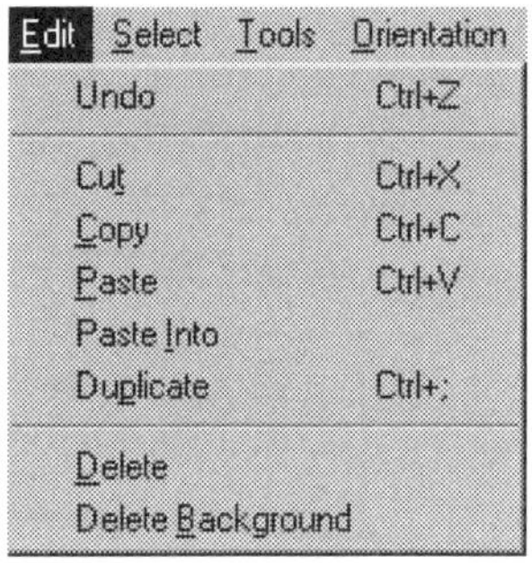

Paste Into is a useful function if you want to perform editing techniques such as inserting a new background into an image.

To do this, select the background from the original image. Then select the background in the destination image and select Edit>Paste Into. A similar technique can be done with the collages special effects.

(For more information on selecting items, see Chapter Five. For more information on special effects, see Chapter Eight.)

- Undo. This undoes the last editing action
- Cut. This removes a selected item and places it onto the clipboard
- Copy. This copies a selected item and places it onto the clipboard
- Paste. This inserts the contents of the clipboard at the selected point
- Paste Into. This can be used to paste the contents of the clipboard into a specifically selected area of another image
- Duplicate. This makes a copy of an image or selected area without first placing it onto the clipboard
- Delete. This removes a selected item or area
- Delete Background. This removes everything except a selected item or area

Toolbars

The toolbars offer options for opening images, editing them, creating special projects and sharing them over the Internet. Each toolbar consists of graphical buttons and each one can be selected to see the sub-options that are available. For some, such as the guided activities, there is a step-by-step procedure for creating the desired effect.

For more on opening images, see Chapter Two.

Click here to see the options for each of the toolbars

Click on a button to see the available sub-options

The Print button offers several options for printing the current active image. These include printing multiple copies of the same image on a page and printing T-shirt transfers.

Get & Fix Photo toolbar

This is used to open images from a variety of sources and perform several editing techniques:

Open images from a variety of sources

Edit the colour quality

Add special effects

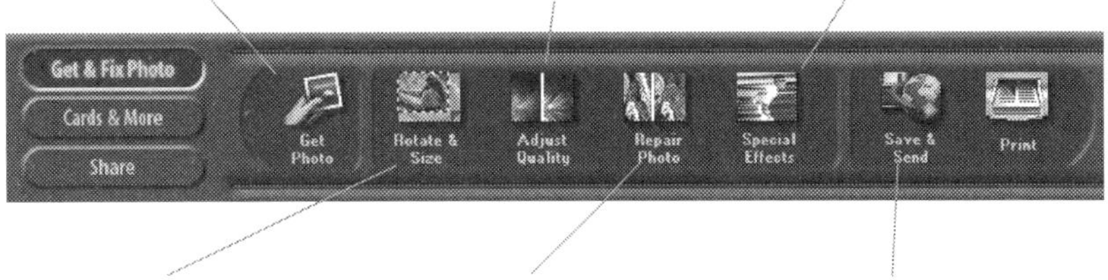

Change the size or orientation

Remove blemishes or entire items

Save a file, save it on the Web or send it as an email

The Save & Send and the Print options are also available on the Cards & More toolbar (see next page).

Cards & More toolbar

This is used for special projects such as producing cards or calendars, or creating on-screen slide shows:

To complete these special projects, click on the relevant button and then follow the step-by-step instructions.

The second option on the Share toolbar is for Seasonal Activities. These are pre-designed templates and images that can be used according to a particular season. These can be loaded from the PhotoDeluxe CD-ROM and then an installation screen will appear at the appropriate time of year. Follow the on-screen instructions to install the activities for the appropriate season.

Share toolbar

This enables you to use your images on the Web in a variety of ways and email them to people:

The Seasonal Activities are dependent on your PC's date and time settings.

File formats

There are dozen of file format in which images and graphics can be created. For images that are going to be viewed on the Web or sent via email the two most commonly used are:

- JPEG (Joint Photographic Experts Group)
- GIF (Graphical Interchange Format)

Both of these create clear images while still managing to keep the overall file size relatively small. GIFs use 256 colours and are best for images that do not have a lot of definition, such as graphics and logos. JPEGs on the other hand can use up to 16 million colours and so are a more popular choice for photographic images. However, despite the apparent difference in the number of colours used, GIFs can also be used for photographs and the quality can sometimes be similar to that of a JPEG.

Both JPEGs and GIFs can be used for images that are going to be printed, as can a variety of other image formats. One useful one for printing is TIFF (Tagged Image File Format) because it offers good quality and file compression and can also be used in PC and Mac formats.

If you select Save when you have finished editing an image then it will automatically be saved in a PhotoDeluxe file format. This is also true for Save As since this just changes the file name rather than the file format.

If you want to save an image into another format, select File>Export> File Format and then select the format into which you want to save the image. If you do this, the PhotoDeluxe file which will still be open can then be closed. The changes do not have to be saved, because this has already been done when the file was exported to a different format.

Proprietary formats

Some image editing programs use their own specific file formats and PhotoDeluxe is no different. Whenever it opens an image it does so in its own format, which has a file extension of '*.pdd' , or '*.pbd'. This means that the original file is untouched — the file that PhotoDeluxe has created is a copy of the original that has been converted into a proprietary format. To denote that the current image has been opened in the PhotoDeluxe format, the following icon appears next to the file name:

Memory issues

In order to try and save memory when editing images in PhotoDeluxe, try and make the original images as compact as possible.

When dealing with any form of digital image, memory is always an issue. To some extent this includes the hard disk space on your computer, since if you use a lot of large digital images then you could eventually run out of space. However, with disc space now being measured in gigabytes these days you will have to store thousands of images before this becomes a problem.

When working with images, always save your work regularly (at least every 15 minutes). This is because they are so memory hungry that image editing programs can, and do, crash quite a lot.

The real issue with memory is with RAM (Random Access Memory). This is the part of the computer that performs the calculations and tasks chosen by the user i.e. editing images or converting them into a different file format. Image editing is very memory hungry as far as RAM is concerned and it is frequently the case that a lot more RAM is required for editing purposes than the actual file size of the image. For instance, if you have an image that is 1 Mb, you may require 5 Mb of RAM for editing purposes.

The scratch disc is a type of virtual memory that PhotoDeluxe uses when the available RAM is used up. If the scratch disc is used up too then you will not be able to continue.

In order for PhotoDeluxe to run as efficiently as possible, make sure that you have a minimum of 32 Mb of RAM installed on your computer. In addition to this, PhotoDeluxe also uses a device called a scratch disc to boost the memory used for editing. It is also possible to assign more of your machine's available RAM to PhotoDeluxe. To do this:

1. Select File>Preferences>Memory Preferences from the Menu bar

2. Enter a value for the amount of available RAM that PhotoDeluxe should use. This should not be more than about 75%

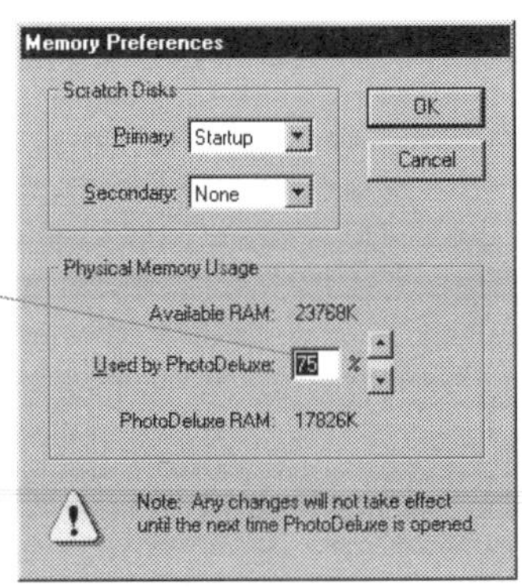

If the amount of RAM allocated to PhotoDeluxe is more than 75% then this may cause problems when performing tasks that are not directly related to image editing in PhotoDeluxe.

Working with images

Images can be obtained from a variety of sources for PhotoDeluxe. This chapter looks at the methods available and how images can be opened in PhotoDeluxe.

Covers

Chapter Two

Obtaining images

An image editing program like PhotoDeluxe is of little use unless it has some images to edit. These can either be obtained from a source such as a CD-ROM or they can be captured with a device such as a digital camera. Wherever an image comes from, the process for opening it is the same:

1 Select Get & Fix Photo>Get Photo

2 Select the source from where the image will be obtained

Images in a non-digital format have to be converted to a digital one before they can be used in PhotoDeluxe. This can either be done by using a scanner or taking them to a photographic shop that specialises in digital images. They will then convert your images into a digital format by putting them on a CD-ROM.

All images that are edited in PhotoDeluxe are digital ones. These can either be in a digital format to begin with or they can be converted from a hard copy format.

Digital formats

Images in a digital format include ones that have been obtained from:

- A floppy disc or Zip disc
- A CD-ROM
- The Web
- A digital camera
- A scanner

Non-digital formats

Images in a non-digital format can be film prints, transparencies or negatives. In each case they have to be converted to a digital format, usually with a scanner.

Images from the hard drive

Images already stored on a hard drive can easily be opened in PhotoDeluxe and this is probably the quickest way to acquire an image. To do this:

1 Select Get & Fix Photo>Get Photo> Open File

2 In the Open dialog box, locate the required file from your computer's hard drive. Select Open

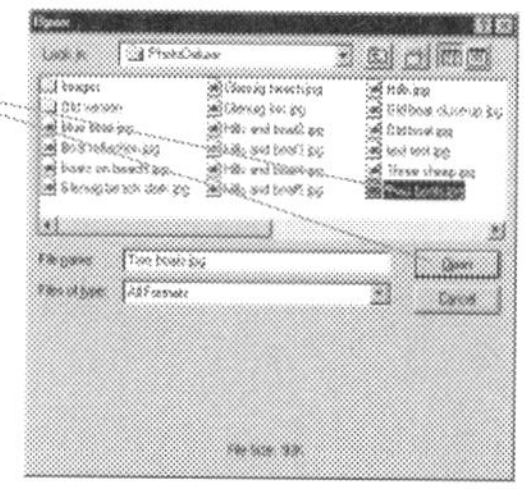

Graphics, such as clip art and icons can be opened in PhotoDeluxe in just the same way as photographic images. This can be useful for creating items such as logos or customised graphics.

3 Even though the file has been accessed from the hard drive, it is opened as a new, untitled, file in PhotoDeluxe

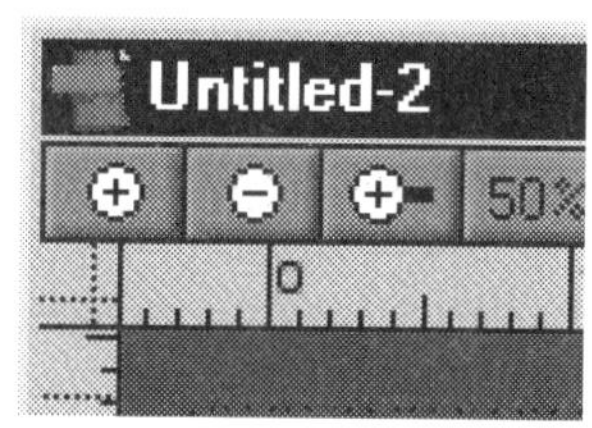

4 Select Save or Save As in the File menu to save the file in a proprietary PhotoDeluxe format

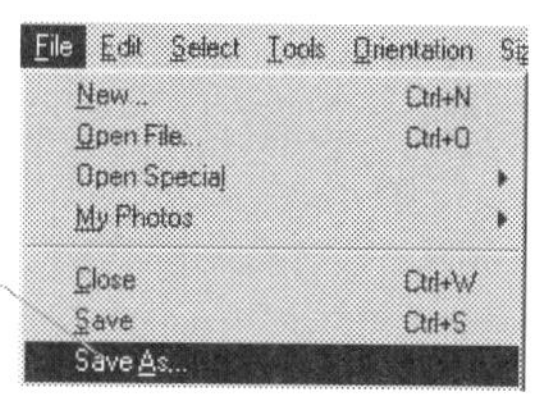

5 Select File>Export to save the file in another format, such as JPEG, GIF or TIFF

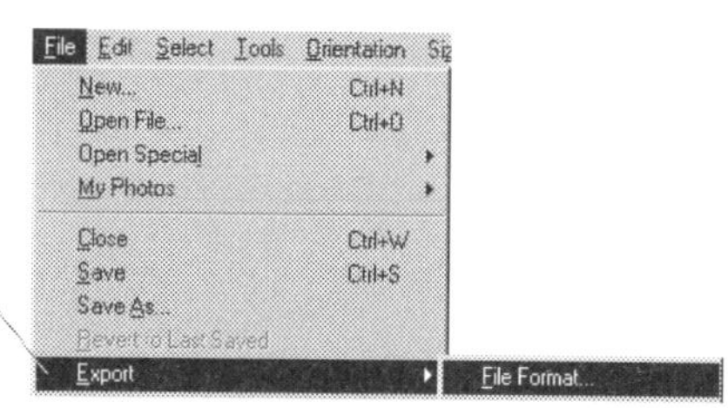

Images from My Photos

In PhotoDeluxe, images can be created and stored in specific folders. This is a useful way in which to organise your images as you will soon find that you have numerous different categories.

To create a new My Photos album

Albums that have been created in ActiveShare can also be accessed through the My Photos option. For more information on ActiveShare, see Chapter Eleven.

1 Select Get & Fix Photo>Get Photo

2 Select My Photos

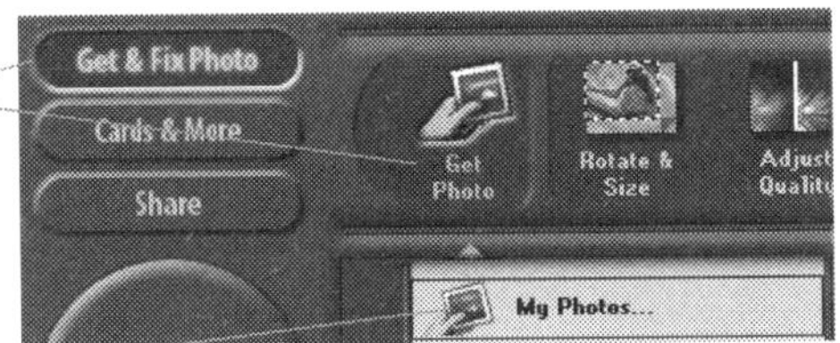

3 Select the New Album button

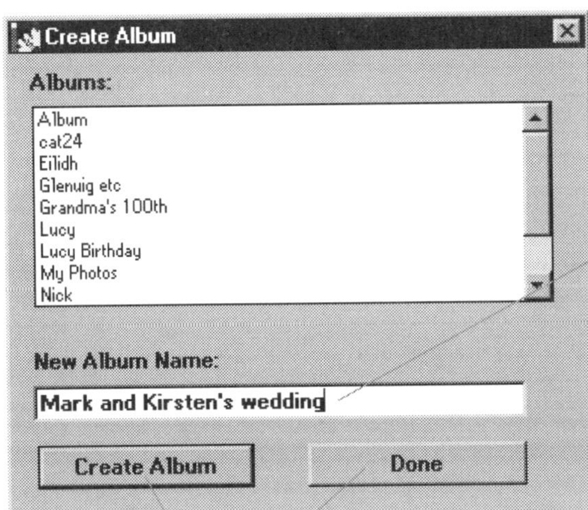

4 Enter a name for the new album

5 Select Create Album and then Done

Opening images from My Photos

1. Select Get & Fix Photo>Get Photo

2. Select My Photos

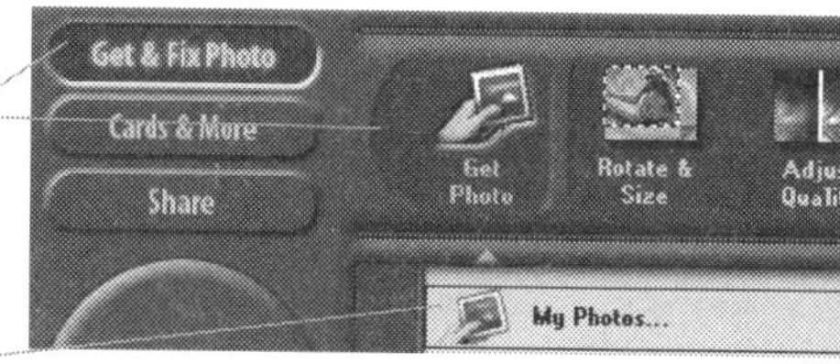

3. Select a current album. Click on these arrows to move through the available albums

To search for a particular image, select the Find Photos button in the My Photos dialog box. In the Find dialog box, enter the filename or caption of the image which you are looking for. Click OK and all of the matching images will be displayed. However, this will only be for the selected album and not all of the albums within My Photos. To do this, each album would have to be selected individually.

4. Thumbnails of the images within an album will be displayed. Double-click on one to open it in PhotoDeluxe

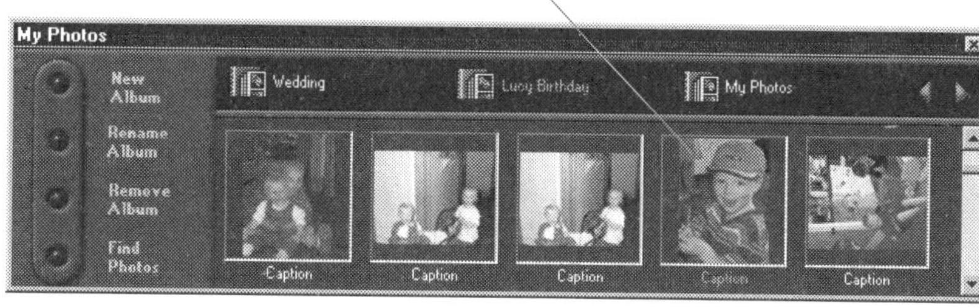

Images from removable discs

If a digital camera has a floppy disc as its image storage device then this limits the size of image that can be captured. A capacity of 1.4 Mb can contain a few images at a low resolution but it is not really suitable for capturing high resolution images.

Floppy discs

The humble floppy disc is fast becoming the poor relation of the digital data storage world. With a modest 1.4 Mb capacity it is not best placed to store even a moderate number of digital images. Some early consumer range digital cameras used floppy discs to store the images that were captured and although one or two on the market still use this method it has been surpassed by smaller memory cards that can hold a minimum of 4 Mb of data.

However, floppy discs still have a number of advantages:

- They are cheap
- They are relatively robust and, due to their size, not as easy to lose as some of the miniature digital camera memory cards
- They offer an easy way to transfer data between computers, since most users have a floppy disc drive on their machine. The exception to this is the iMac from Apple which has no floppy disc drive

Zip discs require their own drive to operate from. These can either be internal or external.

Zip discs

Zip discs are essentially the successors to floppy discs. They are slightly thicker and wider than a floppy and hold a minimum of 100 Mb. Some versions hold 250 Mb and this is fast becoming the standard for this form of storage.

This added storage capacity makes Zip discs ideal for storing and transferring digital images.

For both floppy discs and Zip discs the process for opening images in PhotoDeluxe is the same:

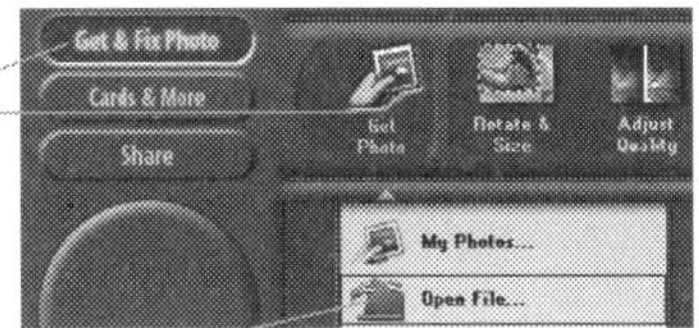

1 Select Get & Fix Photo>Get Photo

2 Select Open File

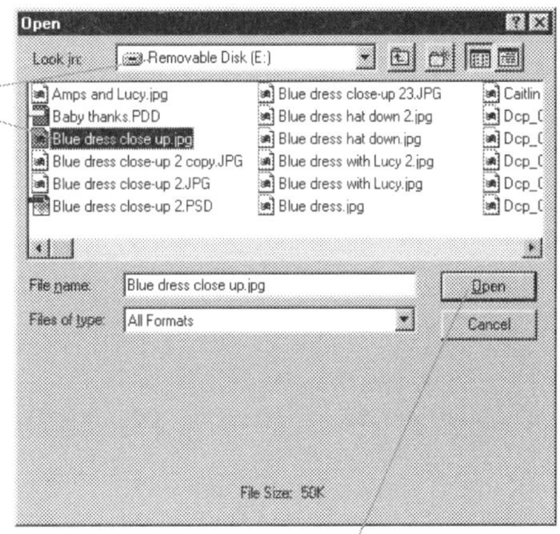

3 Locate an image from either the floppy disc or the Zip disc by clicking on Look in, to find the relevant drive. The drive for the floppy disc will probably be 'A' and the drive for the Zip disc will probably be 'E'

Opening images from discs can be considerably slower than opening them from your computer's hard drive.

4 Select Open

5 The selected image appears on screen

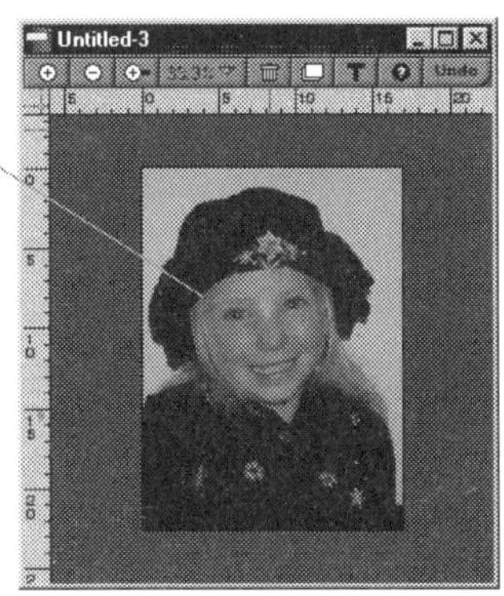

Images from CD-ROMs

Since CD-ROMs have a storage capacity of 650 Mb they are ideal for storing high quality digital images which have large file sizes. These can be obtained by three main methods:

- A Kodak Picture CD
- The CD-ROM that comes with the PhotoDeluxe program
- A CD-ROM that has been created using a CD writer

For more details about Kodak and some of the digital imaging services they offer, look at their Websites at:

- *http://www.kodak.com*
- *http://www.kodak.co.uk*

Kodak Picture CDs

Kodak Picture CDs are images that are put onto a CD-ROM when a roll of film is developed. They can only capture images at one resolution (1024x1536 pixels) and once a roll of film has been added to a Picture CD no more images can be added. PhotoDeluxe displays the images from a Picture CD as thumbnails and then stores them so that they can be opened from the CD.

Kodak Photo Picture CDs can be ordered when a 35 mm roll of film is sent for processing. Specify the type that is required when the film is handed in. (The processing must be done by a Kodak laboratory.) It costs approximately an extra £3 to have a roll of 36 exposures put onto a Picture CD as well as receiving hard copies.

PhotoDeluxe CD-ROM

This can be used to display stock images and also images for seasonal activities.

Recordable CD-ROMs

Until even two or three years ago, it was a complicated and expensive business to copy digital data onto CD-ROMs yourself. But with the development of CD-Writers this is now becoming commonplace. This is an excellent way to store images, since CD-ROMs hold 650 Mb of data. CD-Writers cost in the region of £150, but this is falling all the time and it may soon be the case that they are a standard accessory to most PCs.

To obtain an image from a Kodak Picture CD or CD-ROM:

1. Select Get & Fix Photo>Get Photo

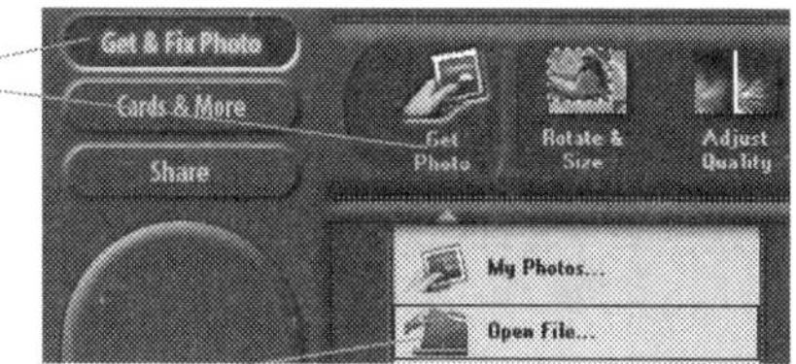

2. Select Open File (or Kodak Picture CD for this type of media)

If you are using a Kodak Picture CD, the images will appear as thumbnails. Double-click on one to see it at full size. More information on creating and using Kodak Picture CDs can be found on the Kodak Websites, see the facing page.

3. Select Look in and select the drive for the CD-ROM (this is usually the D drive)

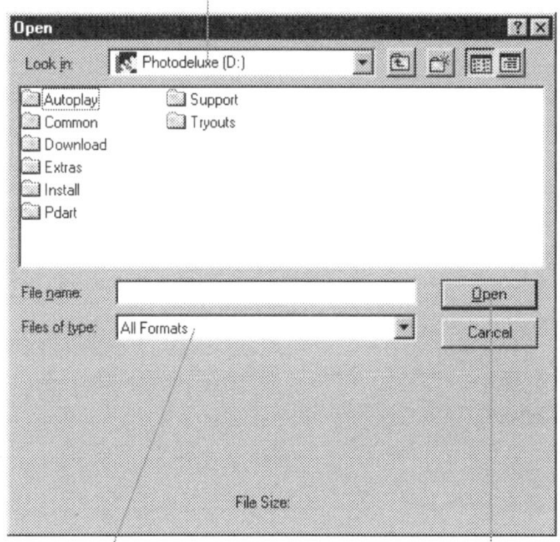

Since CD-ROMS can hold up to 650 Mb of data, the images that are held on them can be very large. This can lead to them taking a long time to open and it can cause problems if you do not have enough memory on your system.

4. Select Files of Type and select the relevant type for the CD

5. Click OK

Images from digital cameras

For a detailed look at digital photography, take a look at 'Digital Photography in easy steps', in the Computer Step range.

Digital photography is a medium which is becoming increasingly popular as it offers the opportunity to create photographic images without the need for traditional film. This is done by capturing a digital image within a camera and then transferring it to a computer where it can be edited using a program such as PhotoDeluxe. The result can then be printed on photographic paper to create the final image. However, as with every type of new technology there are advantages and disadvantages to this latest digital revolution.

Advantages

- Images can be viewed as soon as they are taken, using an LCD panel at the back of the camera. This enables the photographer to immediately delete any images they do not like
- Savings can be made on processing costs since there is no need to buy traditional film or pay to get the pictures developed
- Most digital cameras can hold more than 24 or 36 shots

Images in a digital camera are stored on a memory card which looks like a miniature floppy disc. They come in a variety of sizes, from 4 Mb to 64 Mb. Depending on the size of images that are captured, a 4 Mb card can hold approximately 30–40 images.

Disadvantages

- Digital cameras are not cheap, although the prices are falling rapidly
- Printing costs per image can be high. Ink and special paper can contribute to a cost of 50p–£1 per print
- The technology is changing constantly, so what is state of the art today may seem obsolete in six months' time

Despite the drawbacks, digital photography offers enormous potential for both photographers and computer lovers.

Downloading digital images

Once images have been captured with a digital camera, the next step of the process is to download them onto a computer. This can be done with one of four methods:

Before any images can be downloaded the camera software has to be loaded onto the computer. This is a program that allows the camera and the computer to communicate with each other. In most cases it will be supplied with the camera on a CD-ROM.

- A serial cable connection. This is a cable that connects to the camera and one of the COM ports at the back of the computer. This is a commonly used method, but it is slow and it can be annoying to have to fiddle around with another cable at the back of the computer every time you want to download some images
- USB (Universal Serial Bus) cable connection. This is similar to the first option, except that the cable attaches to the computer's USB port. This speeds up the downloading time considerably but not all older computers are fitted with USB ports
- Card reader. This is a small device that connects into the COM port of the computer. The camera's memory card is then placed in the card reader and the images are downloaded from here
- Infrared transfer. This is a relatively new development that downloads images using infrared signals between the camera and the computer. Both devices have to be IrDA (Infrared Data Association) compliant to use this method. It works by placing the camera in front of the computer's infrared transceiver and then downloading the images. It downloads the images at a similar rate to cable transfer but there are no cables to worry about

If you are going to be downloading a lot of images regularly then it would be advisable to use the USB method of transfer if possible.

Digital images can be downloaded and then stored in a folder on the hard drive for use at a later date, or they can be opened directly in PhotoDeluxe.

To obtain images from a digital camera:

1 Select Get & Fix Photo>Get Photo

2 Select Cameras

If you cannot download your images from your digital camera into PhotoDeluxe, make sure that the camera is turned on and set to Connect.

3 Select the Camera tab and the relevant camera model

4 Select Open Camera

Downloading digital images is never quick, even if you are using a USB connection. If you are downloading more than a dozen images, set the process in operation and then go and make a cup of tea.

5 Select the images that you want to download. Select Transfer to download a specific image, or Transfer All to download all of the images in the camera

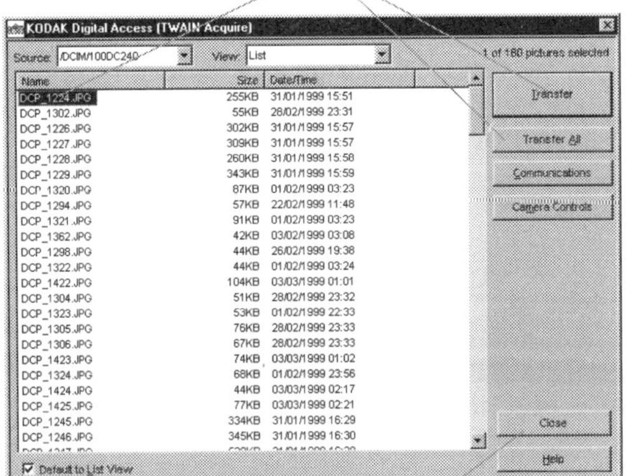

Once you have downloaded images from a digital camera it is still necessary to save them to a location on your hard drive. When you do this, use the Save As command so that you can give the images a meaningful name rather than the numerical value that they are given in the camera.

6 Select Close once you have finished downloading

Images from scanners

Scanners are similar to digital cameras except that they capture a digital image of an existing hard copy item, such as a traditional photograph or a negative. Scanners have come down dramatically in price in the last ten years and they are frequently included as a bundled package with PCs these days. The three main options to look at are:

When buying a scanner, or a digital camera, make sure that it comes with TWAIN compliant software. This enables the scanner or the camera to communicate with the computer and allows images to be opened directly into image editing programs. Most editing software currently on the market is TWAIN compliant.

- Flatbed scanner. This is the most common type and one can be bought for as little as £50, although the quality of the final image will not be as good as a higher specification model. This type of scanner usually copies up to A4 size and they work in a similar way to a photocopier: the image to be copied is placed on a glass plate and then a light source is passed over it. The reflective image is captured on a Charge Coupled Device (CCD). This can then be copied onto a computer. The resolution of flatbed scanners is measured in dots per inch (dpi) and for a good quality scan you should be looking for something in the range of 600 dpi or above

Some scanners come with both flatbed and sheet feed capabilities, but these are more expensive than a single function device.

- Sheet feed scanners. These are scanners that allow for an A4 sheet, or smaller, to be passed through the device in a similar way to a fax machine
- 35 mm film scanners. This is an essential option if you have a lot of 35 mm transparencies that you want to convert into a digital format. These have an adaptor for the transparencies, which is then attached to the scanner. This type of scanner is more expensive than either flatbed or sheet feed devices (approximately £300 upwards) but they offer excellent quality (usually between 1200 dpi and 2750 dpi)

To obtain images from a scanner:

Images can be scanned directly into PhotoDeluxe, without first having to save them anywhere else.

1 Select Get & Fix Photo>Get Photo

2 Select Scanners

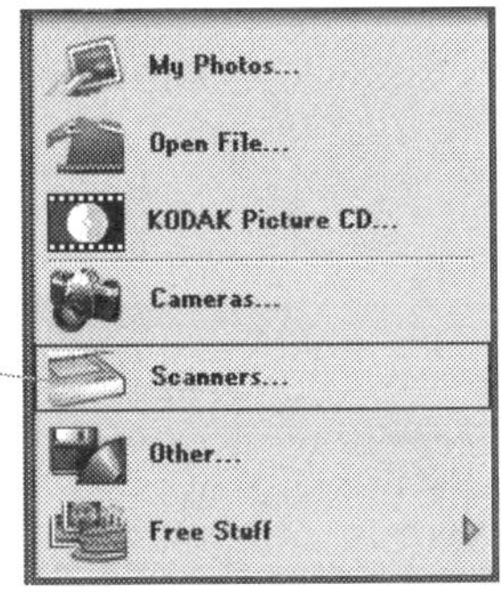

3 Select the Scanner tab and the Choose Scanner button and then the relevant scanner model

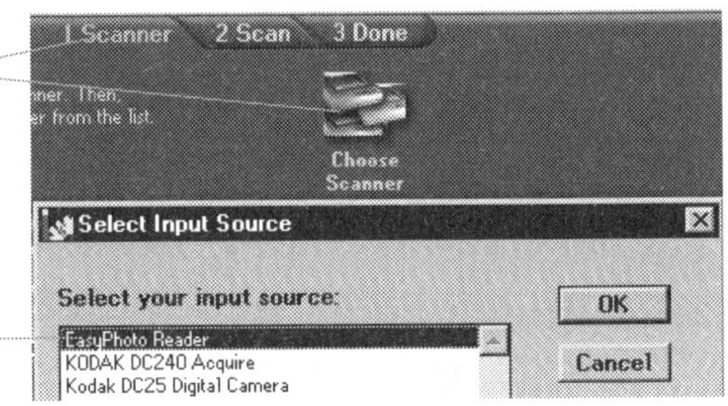

Depending on the quality of the scanner, some of the colours in the image may not be reproduced exactly as in the original. However, it should be possible to improve this during the editing process.

4 Select the Scan tab and the Scan button to have the image scanned directly into PhotoDeluxe

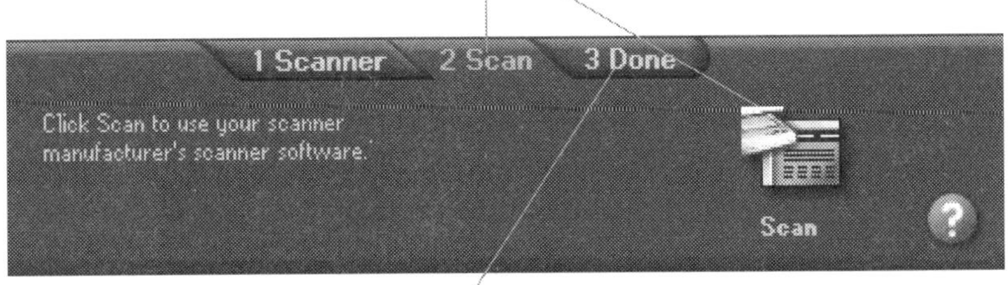

5 Select Done once the image has been scanned

Images from PhotoDeluxe

In addition to creating your own digital items, it is possible to use a variety of images that are provided with PhotoDeluxe (on the installation CD-ROM or from the Website). These can be used to practise your editing techniques, or for inclusion in digital projects.

Do not use any of the images on the PhotoDeluxe CD-ROM for commercial purposes, or you may be infringing copyright.

Sample photographs

PhotoDeluxe provides dozens of images that can be used, for editing practise or simply because you like the pictures, and some of the photography is stunning. To access these:

1 Select Get & Fix Photo> Get Photo

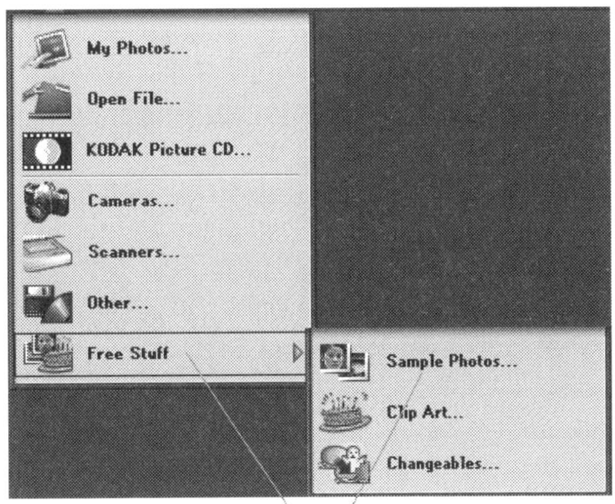

2 Select Free Stuff>Sample Photos

3 Insert the PhotoDeluxe CD-ROM, click on a category and double-click on an image to open it

If you are inserting clip art into documents, use it sparingly as a little can go a long way.

Clip art

This is the same as for the sample photographs, except select Free Stuff>Clip Art at Step 2 above.

Changeables

This is a collection of editable clip art that can be customised and then added to other images or projects.

Accessing Changeables

1. Select Get & Fix Photo>Get Photo

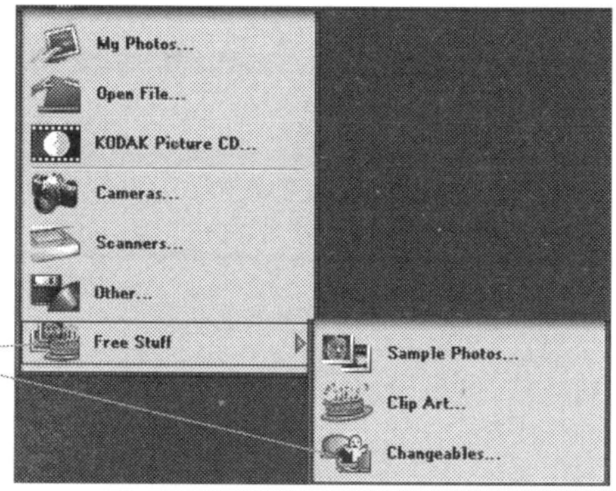

Changeables can only be edited before they are added to an image or project. If you want to change them once they have been inserted you would have to open the Changeable again and undertake the editing process again.

2. Select Free Stuff> Changeables

3. Insert the PhotoDeluxe CD-ROM, click on a category and double-click on an image to open it

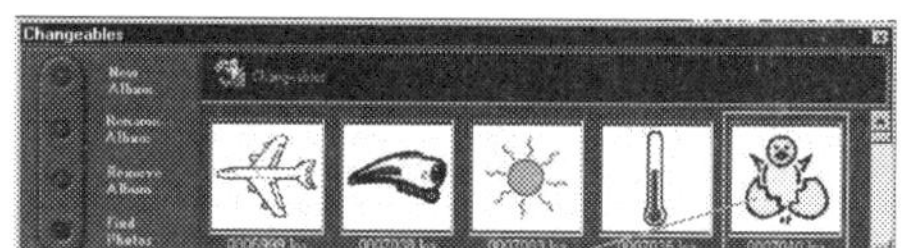

4. Drag the sliders to change the appearance of the image

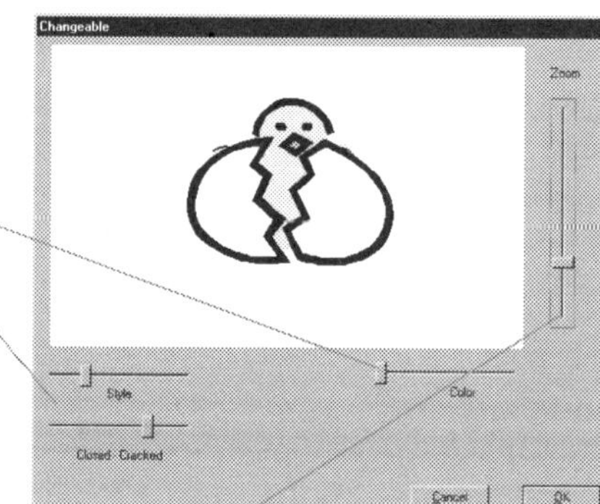

5. Drag the zoom slider to change the size of the image

6. Click OK

Basic editing

One of the advantages of digital images is the ability to edit them on a computer and PhotoDeluxe offers a range of options for improving the appearance and colour of images. This chapter looks at some of the more straightforward editing techniques and shows how they can quickly make significant improvements to an image.

Covers

Chapter Three

Instant Fix

The Instant Fix option is basically a bit of digital guesswork by PhotoDeluxe. It estimates what it thinks the image should look like, but since it cannot see the image itself the results can be a bit hit and miss. This is particularly true for subtle areas of colour, such as skin tones. For these, it is best to edit the colours manually.

For many photographers, the idea of having a single button to correct all of the errors in an image is something of a dream come true. But, to a certain extent, this is exactly what PhotoDeluxe offers with its Extensis Instant Fix Tools. This is an option that automatically edits an image by adjusting elements such as brightness, contrast and colour balance in one operation. There are also Instant Fix options for these items individually.

In certain circumstances, the Instant Fix option can be a quick and effective way to edit images, but there are some drawbacks:

- It is generally less satisfactory than editing each element manually
- It may improve one element of an image to a greater extent than another element
- Unusual lighting conditions and subtle colours may cause problems
- It can lead to shortcuts in the image editing process that result in an inferior final product

Instant Fix is a good way to begin image editing to see how elements such as brightness and contrast change during the editing process. However, as you get more experienced you may get better results by performing these tasks manually.

When the Instant Fix command is being used it is important to make a copy of the image first, so that you can return to the original if you decide you do not like the changes that you have made with the Instant Fix.

To access the Instant Fix options, select an image and then select the Adjust Quality button on the toolbar:

With an image already imported, click here to access the Instant Fix options

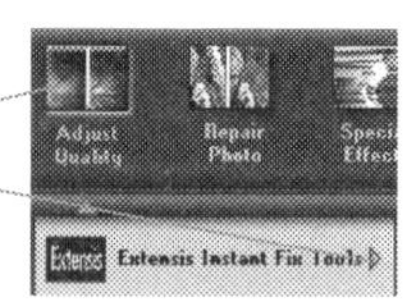

Overall Instant Fix

It is possible to instantly fix all of the colour elements in an image, or select specific items such as brightness and contrast. To apply the Instant Fix command to all of the colour elements in an image:

1. Open the image that you want to edit

2. Select the Adjust Quality button and then select Extensis Instant Fix Tools> IntelliFix Instant Fix

3. Instant Fix will now be applied to the entire image, editing the brightness, contrast and colour balance

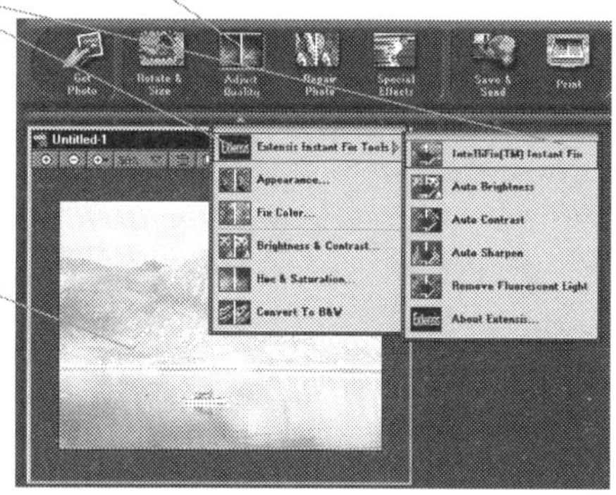

As with any image editing process, it is a good idea to print out an image once Instant Fix has been applied to it. This will give you a chance to see how the editing has affected the printed version of the image.

4. If you do not like the final image, select Undo and then select Quality>Instant Fix from the Advanced Menu bar. This balances the light and dark colours in the image and can give a more subtle effect

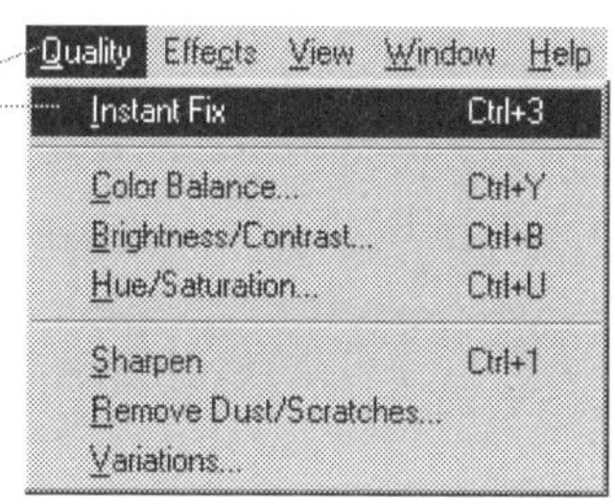

Instant Fix for individual colour elements

Instant Fix can also be applied to separate elements within an image. This can be useful if you feel that most of the image is acceptable but you want to edit one feature such as brightness. Instant Fix can then be applied to this, without affecting other elements of the image. To access the Instant Fix Tools:

1 With an image opened, select Adjust Quality> Extensis Instant Fix Tools

2 The Instant Fix options can then be selected from the following menu:

If an image is badly out of focus then even the most sophisticated Sharpening option will probably not be able to save it. In cases like this, try and recapture the image.

The Instant Fix tools offer the following options:

- Brightness. This adjusts the brightness of colours in an image. It can make them look more vibrant, or paler, depending on the setting
- Contrast. This adjusts the tones in an image i.e. the difference between the light and dark areas
- Auto Sharpen. This applies sharpening to an image, which is a method for improving an image that is slightly blurred or out of focus. This is discussed in greater detail in Chapter Four
- Remove Fluorescent Light. This adjusts the colour balance if it has been adversely affected by fluorescent light. This is usually identified by a greenish tinge

Some digital cameras have settings to compensate for fluorescent light when an image is being captured.

Brightness and contrast

Although the Instant Fix Tools are a quick and, at times, effective way to edit images, a better result can usually be achieved by editing each element individually. This takes a little longer but the results are worth it and it helps to give you a greater understanding of the image editing process and how different operations affect images.

Two of the most common editing techniques involve adjusting the brightness and contrast of an image. This can transform moderate images into striking ones:

When editing the brightness and contrast of an image, make small changes at a time so you can see how the editing process alters the image. However, it is also worthwhile experimenting by applying the maximum levels at each end of the editing scale. This will demonstrate the extremes within which you are operating.

1. An original image that is both too dark and suffering from too low a contrast between the colour tones. In this condition the image would serve little useful purpose

2. The same image once the brightness and contrast have been edited. The colours are now much sharper and the improvement in the contrast has ensured that the image has a lot more depth and texture to it

In PhotoDeluxe the brightness and contrast editing commands can be accessed in two ways.

From the toolbar

If the toolbar is not visible, click on the Get & Fix Photo tab at the top left of the screen.

1 Open an image that requires the brightness and contrast to be edited

2 Click Adjust Quality> Appearance

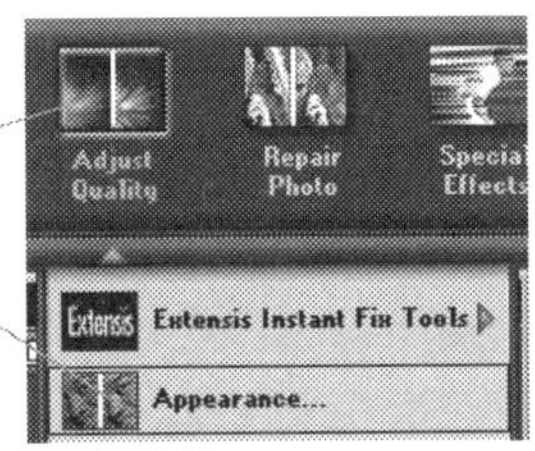

With this method you can choose not to use the Instant Fix if you want. However, you still have to select this step before you can edit the brightness and contrast. Simply ignore it and select the next tab.

3 Select the Instant Fix tab. You can then either apply Instant Fix or select the Tune tab to edit the brightness and contrast manually

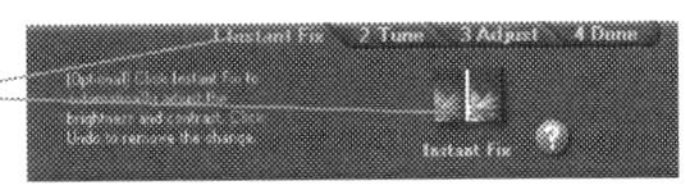

4 Select the Brightness and Contrast button

5 The Brightness and Contrast can then be adjusted in the dialog box (see the facing page)

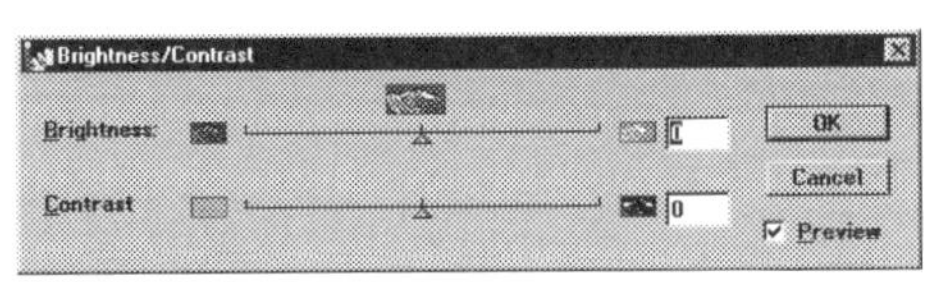

From the Advanced Menus

If the Advanced Menus are not showing, click on the Advanced Menus button at the bottom left of the screen.

1. Open an image and select Quality> Brightness/Contrast

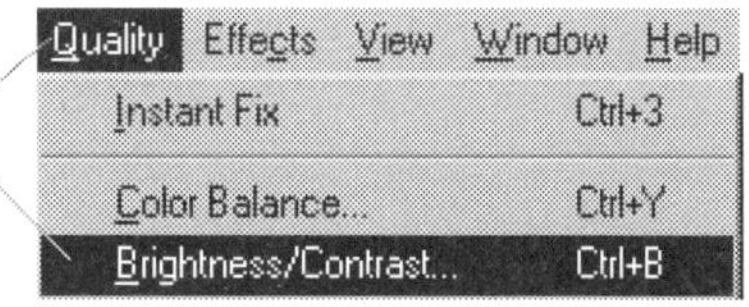

2. In the Brightness/ Contrast dialog box, adjust each value by dragging the sliding scales or adding values into the text boxes

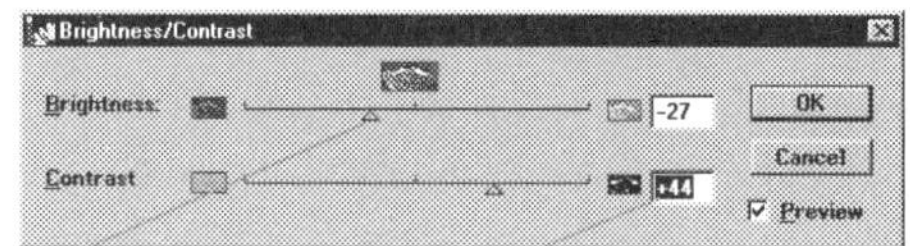

If you set the brightness to its maximum (+100) and the contrast to its minimum (–100), the image will be completely white. If you set the brightness to its minimum and the contrast to its maximum, the image will be completely black.

3. An image with the brightness at +50 and the contrast at –50

4. The same image with the brightness at –50 and the contrast at +50

Colour balance

The colour balance of an image is determined by the relative levels of three pairs of colours: red and cyan; green and magenta; and blue and yellow. The colours in each pair appear opposite each other on a standard colour wheel and you can alter the colour balance by adding or decreasing the amount of a certain colour. So, for instance, if there is too much red in an image you would correct this by adding more cyan.

Correcting the balance

Colour balance can be edited using the Instant Fix Tools but you have more control, and can make more subtle changes, by performing this manually from the Advanced Menus.

The colour balance can be altered by entering numerical values directly into the text boxes in the Color Balance dialog box. If the number is above zero it will move the slider to the right and if it is below zero it will move it to the left.

1 Open an image and select Quality>Color Balance

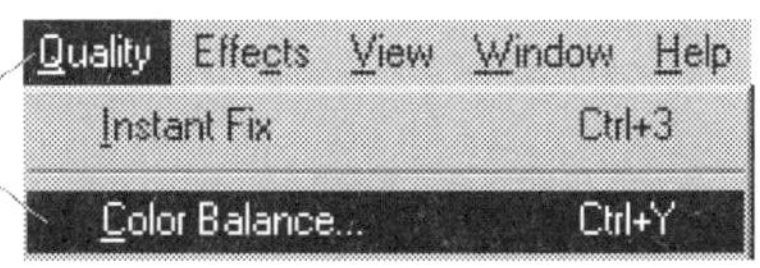

2 To alter the amount of red or cyan, drag this slider or enter a value into the left box

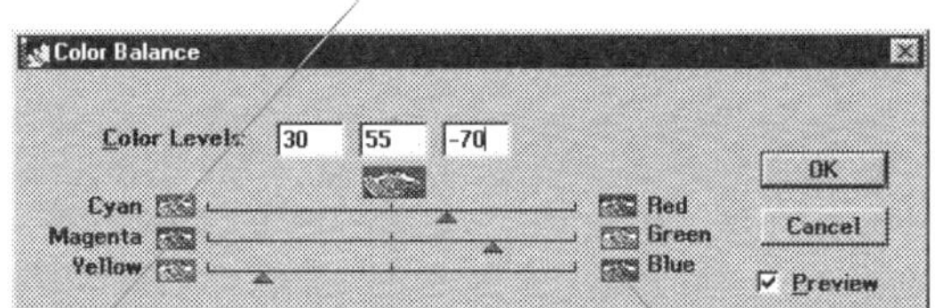

3 To alter the amount of green or magenta, drag this slider or enter a value into the centre box

4 To alter the amount of blue or yellow, drag this slider or enter a value into the right box

Variations

The Variations function gives a visual representation of how altering one element of the colour balance will affect the image. It offers several selections of the image, each depicting how it would appear if more of a certain colour was added. It also shows the original image so you can see what impact your editing changes are making. To access Variations:

You can select each variation option as many times as you like. After each selection the Current Pick image changes accordingly and all of the variations change to show what the next selection would look like. If, at any time, you decide you do not like the changes you have made you can select the Original option, which remains the same throughout. Once you select OK the Original will be replaced by the Current Pick.

1 Open an image and select Quality>Variations

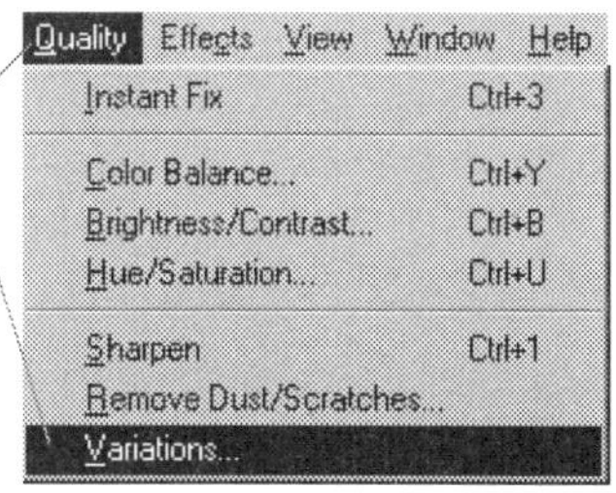

2 The Current Pick is shown here. This is how the image would appear if OK was selected at this point

4 Select OK once you are satisfied with the colour of the Current Pick

3 The colour variations are displayed around the Current Pick. Click on one to add more of that colour. The Current Pick will become updated accordingly

The two Current Pick icons are the same, but note the following:

- *the Current Pick in the middle of the images shows it in relation to the variations nearest to it.*
- *the Current Pick at the top displays how the Current Pick looks compared with the original image*

Cropping and trimming

Even the most experienced photographers frequently capture images that need to be altered before they look their best. One of the most common techniques is cropping and trimming. This involves removing parts of the image so that the main subject is clearer or more prominent. This happens even at the highest level of photography and it should be a natural consideration for most images. Some of the reasons for cropping are:

Unless you have a good reason not to, cropping should be considered for virtually every image you edit.

- To remove a large, bland background that detracts from the main subject
- To remove distracting objects in the background, such as telephone poles or unsightly buildings
- To give a portrait greater impact. This can be particularly effective if it is a facial portrait: by cropping the background, the face can be made to fill the entire image

One reason for not applying cropping is if you want to use an expansive background to give the impression of size and space.

Cropping is a quick and easy way to turn moderate images into excellent ones:

1 In this image the background rather dwarfs the main subject

2 By cropping the background the main subject becomes a lot more prominent

Cropping an image

1 Open an image and decide which areas you want to remove

The Trim option can also be accessed from the Advanced Menu by selecting Quality>Trim.

2 Select Rotate and Size>Trim & Size from the Get & Fix Photo toolbar

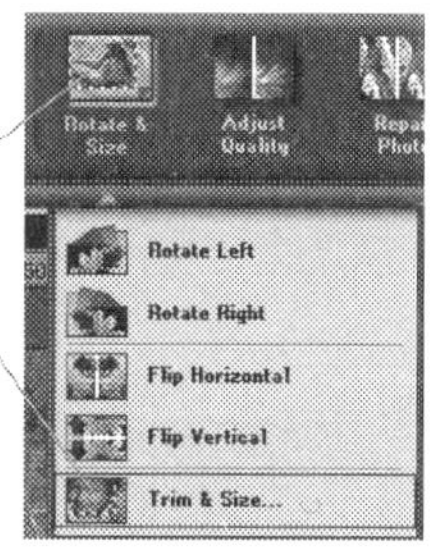

When cropping, it is best to have the whole image visible on screen, so you can see everything you are selecting and removing. A magnification setting of 50% should allow the whole image to be viewed at a comfortable size.

3 Select the Trim tab and then the Trim button and then drag a rectangle around the part of the image you want to keep

4 Select OK and the image is now trimmed to the size of the selection

Noise

Noise in digital imaging terminology refers to the defects that can occur when an image is captured with a digital camera or a scanner. This can cause a number of problems such as graininess, lines across the image and a jagged, blocky effect. PhotoDeluxe has options to remedy most of the problems caused by noise.

Improving graininess

Graininess is usually caused when there is a low level of lighting for a digital camera or a poor quality scanner.

1 Open an image that looks grainy or speckled

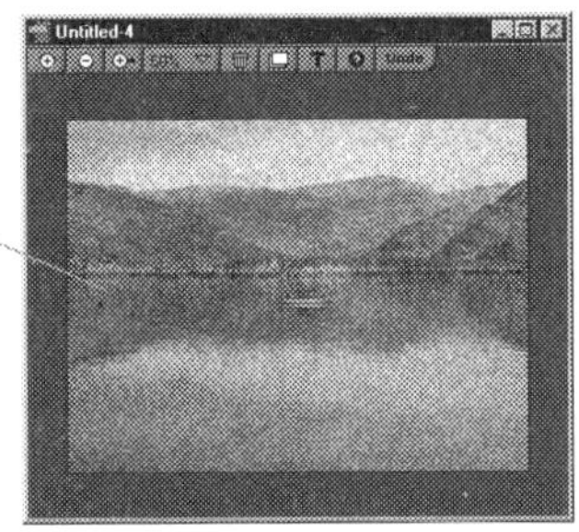

2 Select the Repair Photo button from the Get & Fix Photo toolbar. Select Remove Noise

If you set the Reduce Graininess level too high then the image may become blurred.

3 Select the Graininess tab and then the Reduce Graininess button

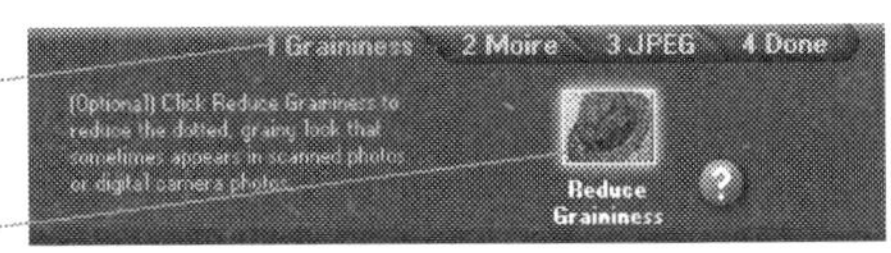

4 Select the zoom level in the Preview box. Then alter the graininess by using the slider or entering a value into the text box

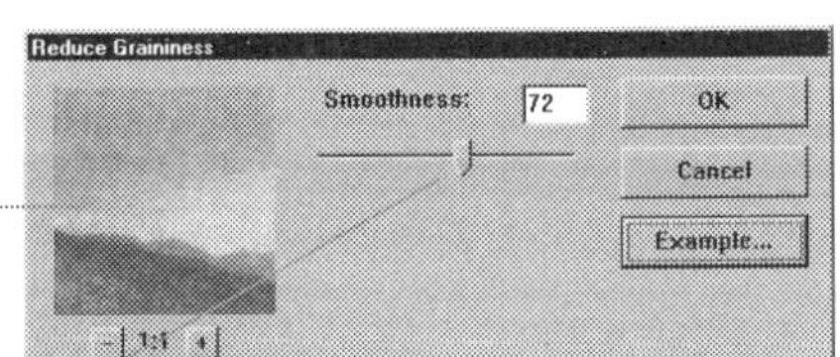

Removing Moiré patterns

Moiré patterns are faint diagonal lines that can cause a crisscross effect on a digital image. This usually occurs when an image is captured on a low quality scanner. To remove Moiré pattern:

The best way to avoid Moiré patterns is to use as good a scanner as possible.

1. Follow the first two steps on the previous page

2. Select the Moire tab and then the Remove Moire button. (To do this, first select the Graininess tab)

3. In the Remove Moire Pattern dialog box, select the angle at which the Moire pattern is affecting your image. Select a level for the smoothness of the editing by using the sliding scale or entering values in the text boxes

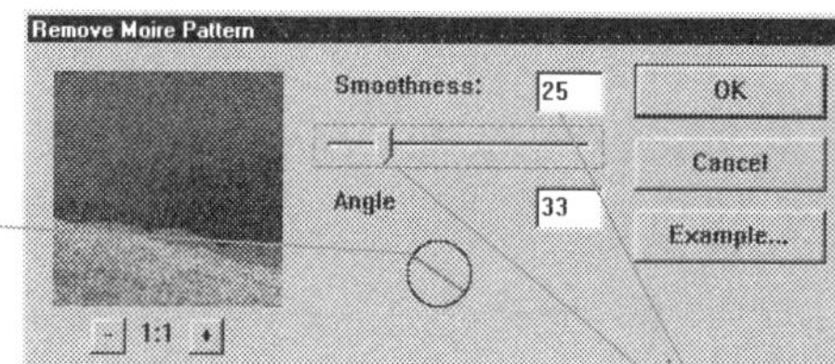

Using Clean Up JPEG

If JPEG images have been enlarged or compressed greatly they can have a jagged appearances, as if each pixel is individually visible. To remove this:

In some quarters, the effect of individual pixels becoming visible is known as 'jaggies'.

1. Follow the first two steps on the previous page

2. Select JPEG>Clean Up JPEG and then adjust the image in the same dialog box on the previous page

Undoing edits

Image editing is not always an exact science and there will be times when a particular technique does not produce the results that you had hoped for. This could involve a change of colour, an element that you have added or removed, or an editing function such as sharpening. Luckily, it is possible to undo the last action you have applied, or go back to the last saved version of the image.

Even when a particular editing technique produces an acceptable result on screen, it may look different when it is printed.

Undoing the last action

If you do not like the result of an editing technique you can undo it using the Undo button, but only if you do so immediately and do not undertake any more editing tasks. To do this:

View the effect of the last performed action and, if you do not like it, click the Undo button on the image toolbar. The image reverts to the way it looked immediately before the last edit

Whenever you save an image, make sure it is of an acceptable quality, because this is the one that you will return to if you then subsequently use Revert to Last Saved.

Revert to Last Saved

If you have performed a number of editing tasks and then decide that you do not like the overall effect you can revert to the last saved version of the image. This is done by selecting File>Revert to Last Saved.

However, any changes that were made before the image was last saved will have become permanent. This is an example of why it is always a good idea to make a copy of an image before you start editing.

Further editing

Chapter Four

This chapter looks at some of the editing techniques that can be used to enhance and transform images. These include reducing the effects of red-eye, improving badly focused images and removing a variety of unwanted objects, ranging from spots to buildings.

Covers

Removing red-eye

Red-eye can be avoided by not firing the flash directly at the subject. Try bouncing it off a ceiling or wall, if possible.

One of the most common, and frustrating, reasons for images captured with a flash being unsatisfactory is red-eye. This is the condition where the light from the flash reflects in the pupils of the subject's eyes, resulting in them having red eyes in the final image. This can spoil the most perfect portrait or turn a family shot into an object of considerable amusement. Although PhotoDeluxe cannot avoid red-eye being created in the first place, it can offer some help in erasing it from the affected image:

1 Open the affected image and zoom in on the red-eye portion of it

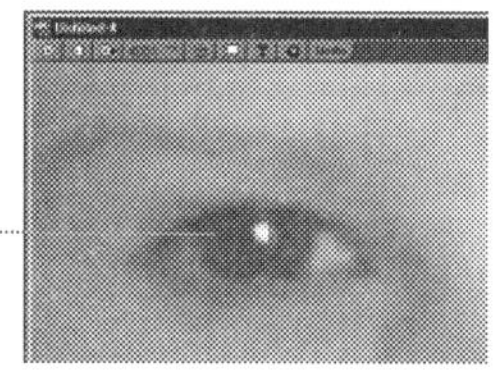

Several digital and conventional cameras have a reduce red-eye option with the flash. This works by flashing once a second or so before the flash for the picture itself is fired. This lessens the effect of red-eye but it does not always remove it altogether. Also, it can create rather unnatural looking images as the subject is either dazzled by the first flash, or else they are looking slightly startled as they await the second one.

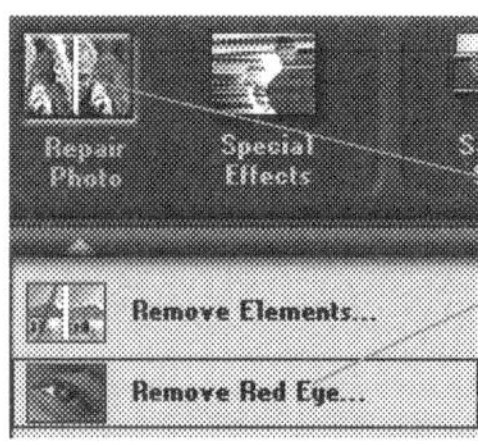

2 Select Repair Photo> Remove Red Eye

3 Click on the Select tab and then the Select Rectangle button. Draw a rectangle around the area affected by red-eye

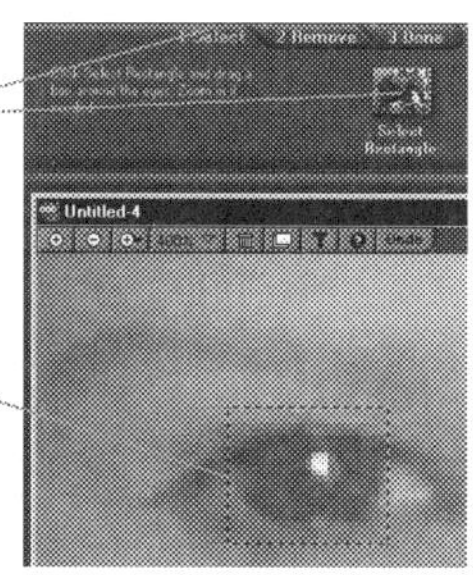

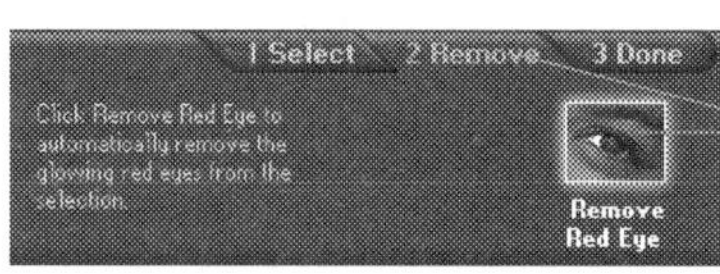

4 Select the Remove tab and then the Remove Red Eye button and then Done. View the result at different magnifications

Sharpening

If you want a hard copy of an image, sharpening is one area where it is essential to print out a draft version to see if this matches the on-screen image. Sometimes a sharpened image can look fine on screen but when it is printed it looks worse than the original out of focus picture. In cases like this, use small levels of sharpening at a time.

Even with the best autofocus cameras on the market it is inevitable that sooner or later you will capture an image that is out of focus. This does not mean that it is necessarily unrecognisable: it may just be a little blurry when examined closely. PhotoDeluxe uses a function known as sharpening to enhance images that are slightly out of focus and give them a clearer appearance. This is done by enhancing the contrast between areas of colour, thus creating the effect of the image being more clearly defined. There are four main options for sharpening:

- Sharpen. This applies the standard level of sharpening
- Sharpen More. This applies a greater amount of sharpening
- Sharpen Edges. This gives greater definition to the edges within the image
- Unsharp Mask. This allows for the sharpening levels to be set manually

Applying Sharpening

There are a number of ways to apply basic sharpening:

Select Adjust Quality>Extensis Instant Fix Tools>Auto Sharpen

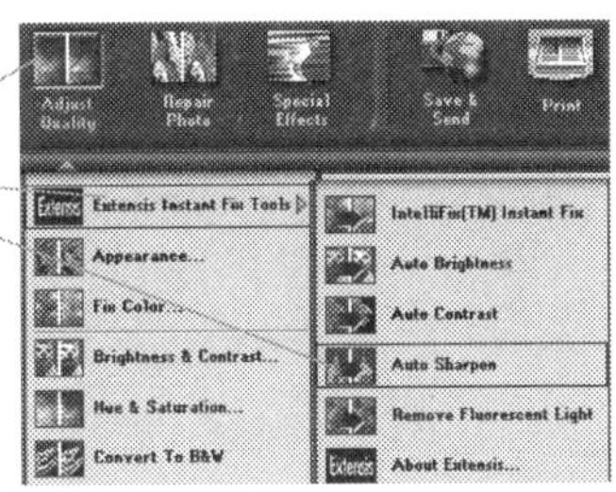

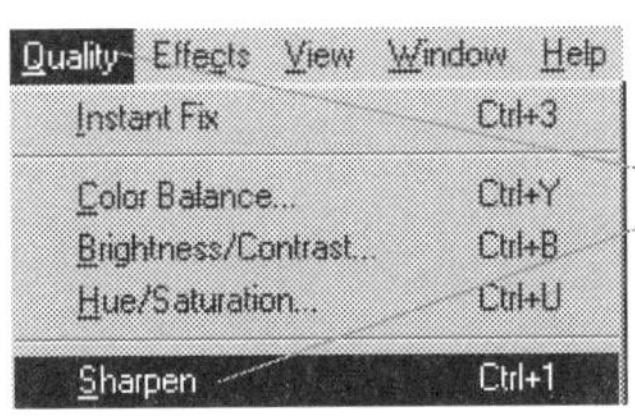

From the Advanced Menus select Quality>Sharpen. Or select Effects>Sharpen>Sharpen

Applying Sharpen More

1. From the Advanced Menus select Effects>Sharpen> Sharpen More

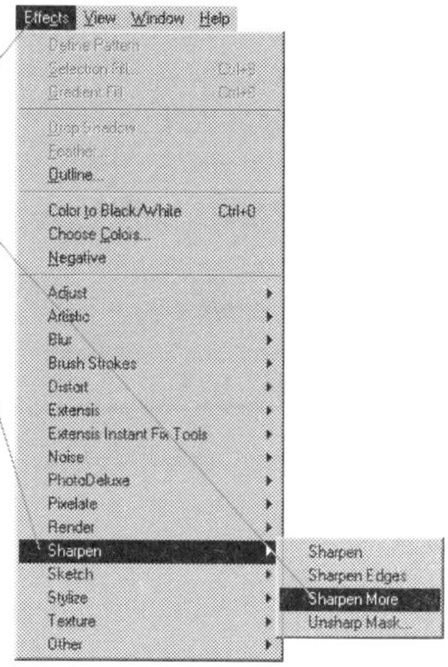

2. This will give an out of focus image the effect of being much clearer

A blurred image that has had sharpening applied to it will not be as clear as a sharply focused original. Use sharpening to remedy minor mistakes rather than using it as an excuse to take shortcuts and capture badly focused images.

Applying Sharpen Edges

1. From the Advanced Menus select Effects>Sharpen> Sharpen Edges

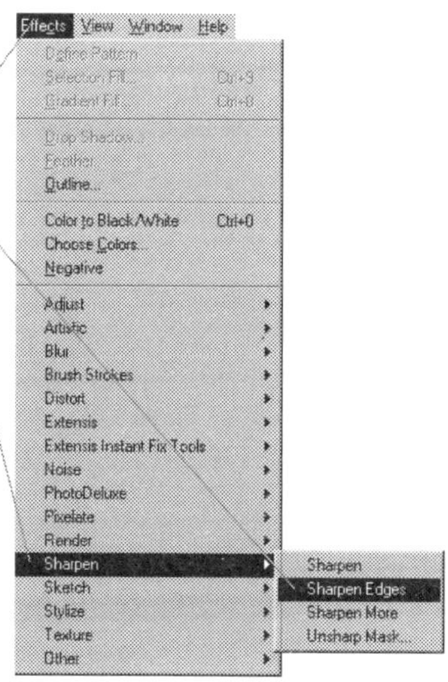

2. This adds extra definition to the edges of an out of focus image

Applying Unsharp Mask

This enables you to apply your own levels of sharpening and it can be useful for an out of focus image and also an image that has become slightly distorted during the editing process. To apply Unsharp Mask:

The default size for the preview box in the Unsharp Mask dialog box is 1:1. However, you can use the + and - buttons to zoom in or out, depending on how big you want the preview image.

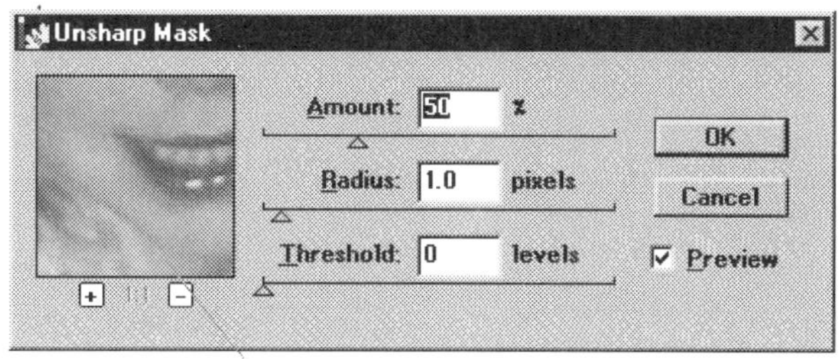

From the Advanced Menus select Effects> Sharpen> Unsharp Mask. This dialog box will appear, with a portion of the image showing so that the changes can be previewed

The Unsharp Mask dialog

If the amount of sharpening is too high then an image may become pixelated i.e. each individual pixel is visible, creating an image with a jagged appearance.

- The Amount determines by how much the contrast between areas of colour is increased i.e. how much sharpening is applied to each pixel. This ranges from 1–500% and for a printed image a level of 150–200% is usually best
- The Radius determines how many pixels next to the edge are affected by the sharpening. This ranges from 0.1–250 and for a printed image a level of between 1–2 is usually best
- The Threshold determines how much contrast there has to be between two pixels before they are considered to be an edge. This ranges from 0–255. The default is 0 and this sharpens all of the pixels in the image. A high threshold level limits the sharpening to areas of high contrast

Cloning

The uses for cloning

Cloning is one of the most versatile and satisfying skills in the digital imaging toolbox. It operates by copying the pixels from one area of an image and then placing them over another. This can be put to a number of uses:

- Removing minor blemishes such as spots and wrinkles
- Removing unwanted items from an image
- Repairing old photographs that are torn and creased

Cloning basics

For all of the uses of cloning the basic technique is the same. For standard cloning:

For the best results, set the image at a high magnification and use a relatively small Clone tool size. If there are a lot of subtle colour changes then clone from several areas within the image.

1 From the Advanced Menus select Tools>Clone

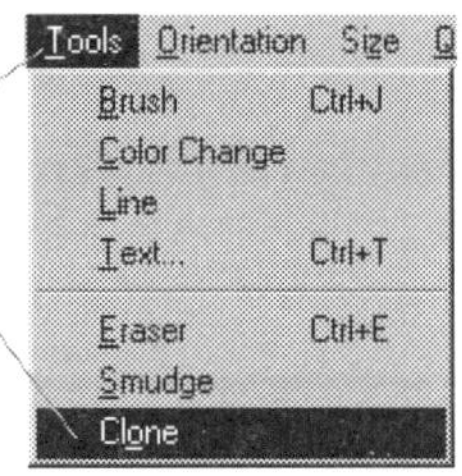

2 Position the source point icon on the part of the image that you want to copy

3 Select a thickness for the Clone tool

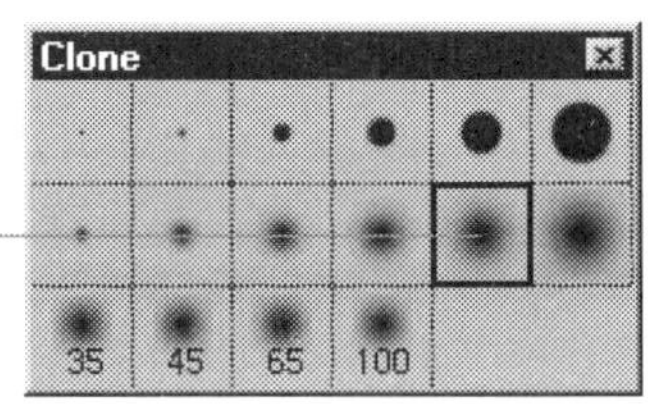

4 The Clone tool is denoted by a circle and a crosshair denotes which area of the image is being copied. Drag the Clone tool over the image to clone it

Removing blemishes

In the world of fashion magazines, photographs of models are frequently touched-up to remove minor blemishes such as moles and small wrinkles. Thanks to PhotoDeluxe this technique is no longer confined to the world of high fashion. To remove minor blemishes such as spots, bags under the eyes or scars:

The source point icon can be moved by clicking on it and then dragging it to a new position.

1 Open an image and select Repair Photo> Retouch Face

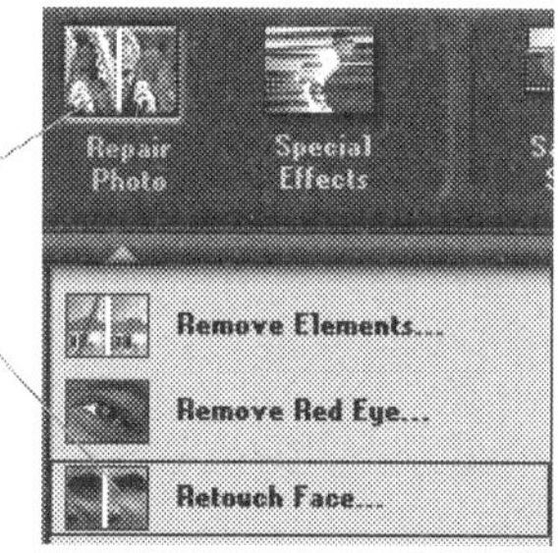

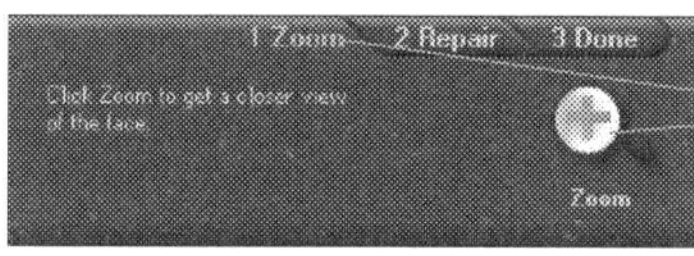

2 Select Zoom. Zoom in by positioning the magnifying glass icon over the affected area and clicking

The source point icon is the starting point for the Clone tool to take colour from. Once you start dragging the Clone tool the colour is then taken from where the source point icon is positioned. So keep an eye on where this is on the screen.

3 Select Repair and click on the Clone button

4 Position the source point icon over the area you want to copy from and select a brush size

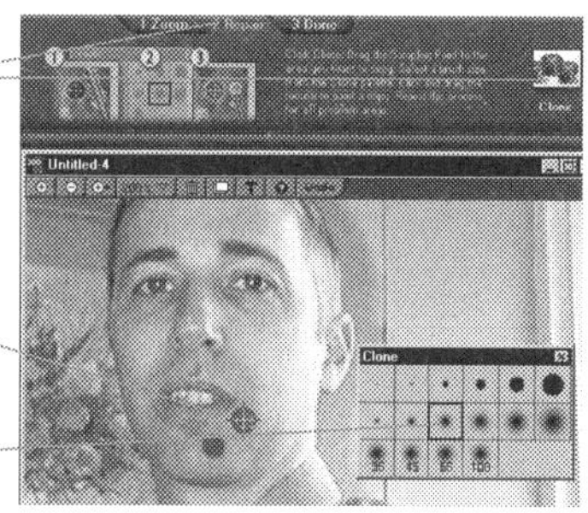

5 Drag the Clone tool over the affected area. If necessary, clone from several areas to get an exact colour match

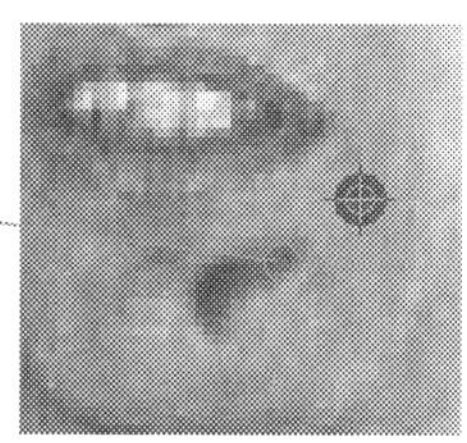

Removing large objects

While it can be satisfying to use cloning to remove small objects such as spots, it can be equally enjoyable to remove larger objects such as buildings or unwanted people. This could be because you want to concentrate on certain people in a group or because a building or object is detracting from the rest of the image. This can be achieved by cloning over the object that you want to remove, in much the same way as you would do with a smaller object. There is also an option for removing the unwanted object and then cloning the subsequent space. To do this:

If you are removing an individual from a group of people it is easiest if they are at an end or the back of the group. Otherwise you could end up with a gap in the image that would have to be filled with something else.

1. Open an image and select Repair Photo> Remove Elements

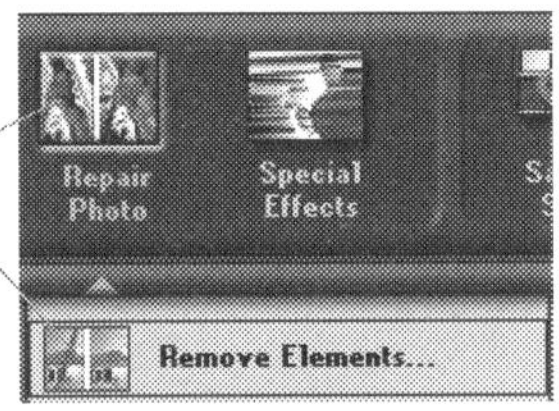

When you are covering a large area with cloning, make sure you move your source point icon regularly. Otherwise you could end up with a symmetrical pattern rather than a smooth cloned area.

2. Click on Select and then the Smart Select button. This enables you to draw an outline around the object that you want to remove. Do this by clicking at the point where you want to begin the selection. Wait until OK appears and then draw an outline around the object that you want contained within the selection. Continue until you have created an outline around the whole object, finishing at the same point where you started. Click on the Wastebasket to remove the selection

For more on selection techniques, see Chapter Five.

3 There will now be a gap in the image, where the selection has been removed

When you are cloning a selected area you cannot work outside this area. If you try to, the Clone tool will not function.

4 Select Cover and click on the Clone button

5 Position the source point icon and select a brush size. Clone the selected area, using a variety of source points if required

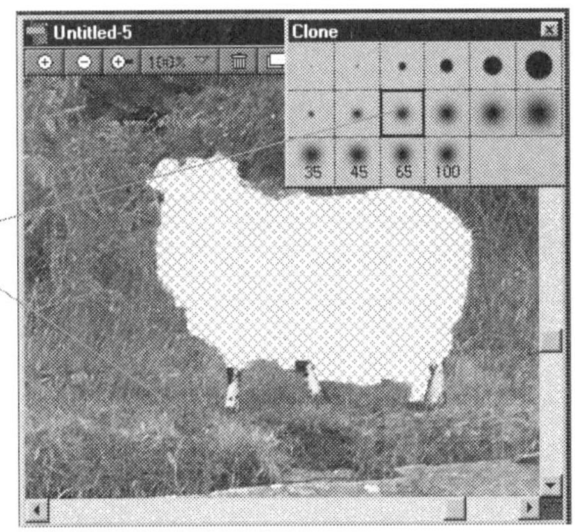

It is possible to remove someone from the middle of a group of people and then move everyone else along to fill in the subsequent gap. Chapter Five gives more details about selecting and moving objects and then cloning any spaces that are left.

6 Select Done. The unwanted object should have now disappeared seamlessly from the image

Repairing old photographs

Another excellent use for cloning is for repairing old photographs that have been torn or become creased over time. This is particularly effective with black and white photographs since the brightness and contrast can also be improved. Capturing a damaged photograph as a digital image can either be done with a scanner or a close-up with a digital camera. If possible, use a scanner since an image captured with a digital camera could be affected with glare from the flash. Once you have an image in a digital format it can then be repaired:

1. Select Repair Photo> Restore Old Photo

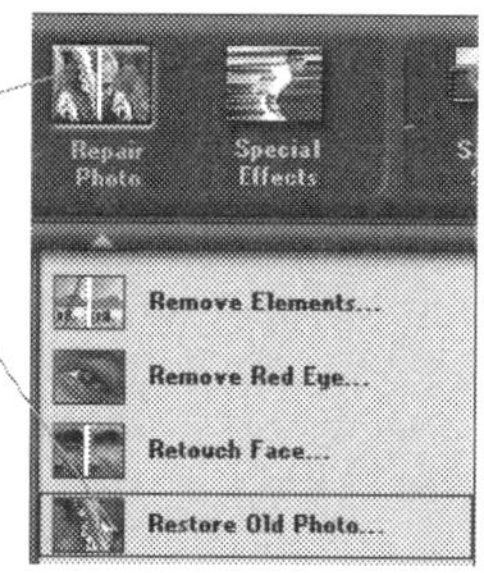

To zoom out from an image, hold down Alt and click. A minus sign should appear within the magnification icon.

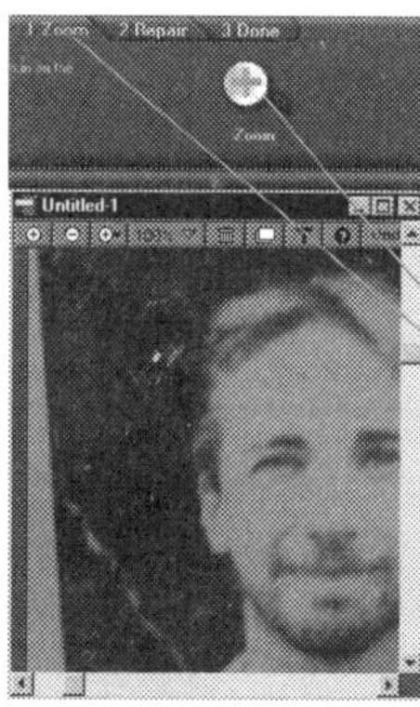

2. Select Zoom and click on the Zoom button. Move the magnification icon to the affected area and click to zoom in

When you have finished repairing all of the tears and scratches, edit the colour and contrast. This will ensure they are at the right levels for the newly repaired image.

3. Select Repair and click on the Clone button. Position the source point icon, select a brush size and then clone the affected area. Repeat this for all of the scratches and tears on the image until it looks clear and sharp

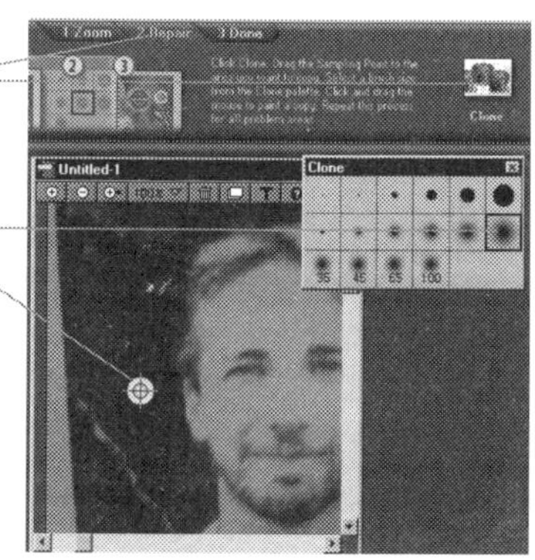

Cloning between images

In addition to cloning areas within the same image, it is also possible to clone an area from one image onto another. This has a similar effect to selecting part of an image and then copying and pasting it, but it can give you more control over exactly what is copied between images. To clone an area from one image to another:

If an area is cloned from one image to another, it is placed on the same level as the rest of the destination image. If an area is selected and then copied and pasted, it will be placed on its own layer. For more information about layers, see Chapter Six

1 Open two images and scale them so that they can be viewed next to each other

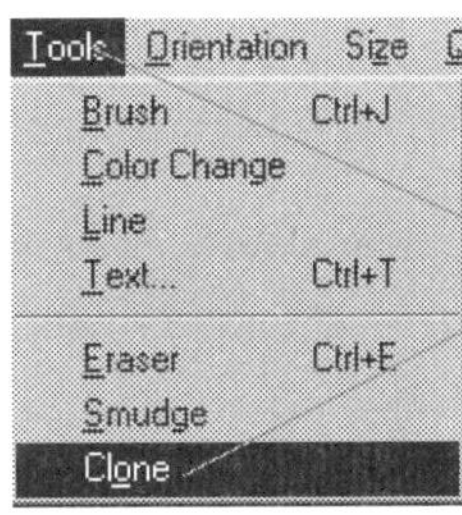

2 Select the Advanced Menus button and select Tools>Clone from the Menu bar

Once you have positioned the Clone tool on the initial image, it does not need to be moved again. If you do move it then the cloned image will not be an exact replica of the original.

4 Drag across the target image to clone the desired area from the first image

3 Place the Clone tool in the middle of the area which you want to copy

Eliminating dust and scratches

Dust and scratches can appear on a digital image for two main reasons: physical impurities that affect scanners and digital cameras or digital imperfections that occur while the image is being captured. One way to avoid this is to make sure your equipment is as clean as possible, which can be done with camera cleaning fluid and a lint free cloth. These can be bought from most camera shops. However, if small blemishes do find their way onto your images they can be removed with the Dust & Scratches option:

The Dust & Scratches dialog box can be accessed through the Advanced Menus by selecting Quality>Remove Dust/Scratches.

1. Open an image and select Repair Photo>Remove Dust & Scratches
2. Click on Select and click on the Select Rectangle button

3. Draw a rectangle around the affected area

4. Select Dust & Scratches and click on the Dust & Scratches button

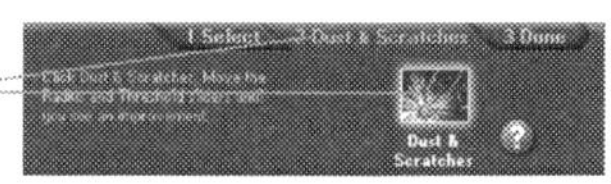

5. In the dialog box, the Radius determines how wide an area is covered when looking for areas of different colour. The Threshold determines the contrast between colours before they are changed. Move the slider for each option until the blemish disappears in the Preview box. Click OK

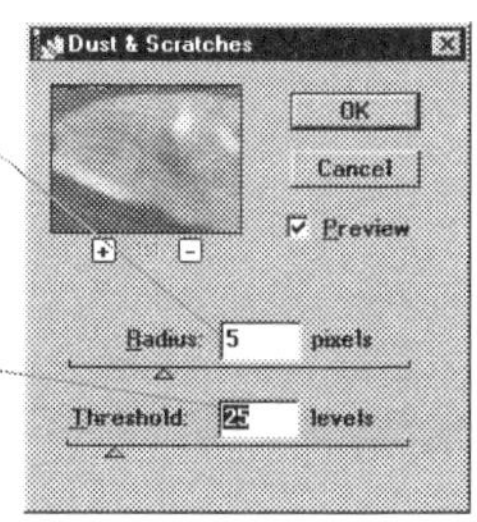

Selecting items

This chapter shows how to use the various tools that can be used to select areas and objects within images. It also demonstrates how selected areas can then be edited, resized or moved.

Covers

Chapter Five

Uses for selections

Unlike traditional photographs, it is possible to select a particular area or item in a digital image and edit it independently from the rest of the image. This could involve enhancing a selection, moving it to another part of the image or deleting it altogether. PhotoDeluxe offers a variety of options for selecting part of an image and some of the uses that this can be put to are:

The range of tools in PhotoDeluxe for selecting an area of an image means that it is just as easy to select an irregular shape as it is to select a symmetrical one.

Selecting the sky in a landscape shot and changing its colour

If items are moved or deleted from an image, then there will be a gap where the item was positioned. The best way to fill this is by cloning, as shown in Chapter Four.

Moving the position of individuals in a group picture

Selecting an item and copying it onto another background

Making a selection

All of the selection tools can be accessed through the Selections dialog box. To make a selection, the initial process is the same for all of the selection tools:

When selecting an area, position the selection tool at the top left-hand corner of the required selection. Click and drag the crosshair cursor down and to the right to capture the selection.

1 If the Selections dialog box is not showing, select View>Show Selections from the Advanced Menus

2 Select a selection tool

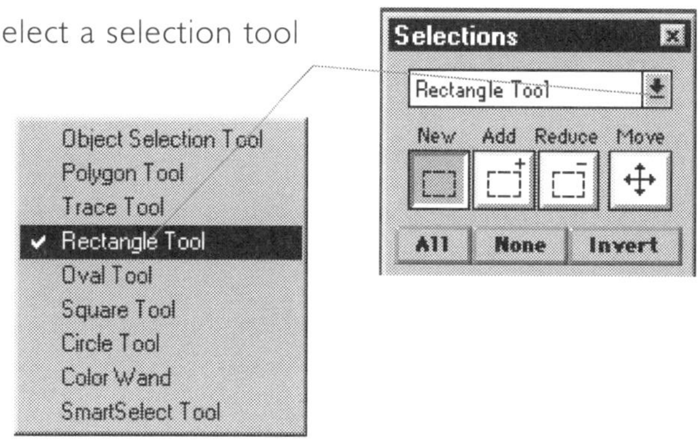

The Selections dialog box can also be accessed by choosing Select> Selection Tools from the Advanced Menus.

3 Position the crosshair cursor over the area you want to select. Click and drag the cursor until it covers the desired selection

4 Any editing functions now chosen will only apply to the selected area

Making symmetrical selections

Use the Rectangle, Oval, Square or Circle selection tools to make symmetrical selections. Each one creates a selection corresponding to its title:

Rectangle

Follow steps 1-2 on page 71 to launch the menu shown here.

Click here and then make a rectangular selection on the image

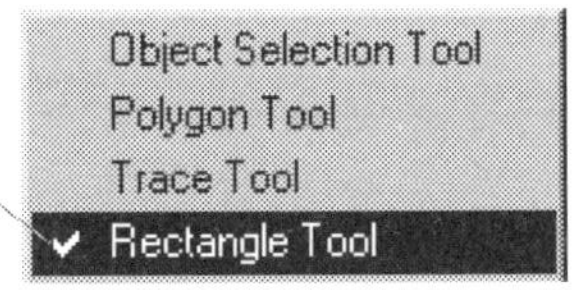

If, after having made a selection, you decide you have chosen the wrong part of the image, you can remove the selection by clicking None in the Selections dialog box.

Oval

Click here and then make an oval selection on the image

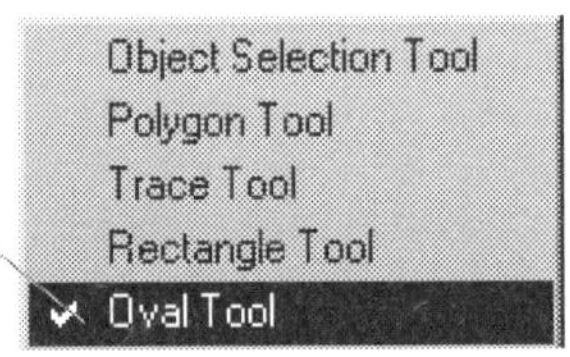

Square

Click here and then make a square selection on the image

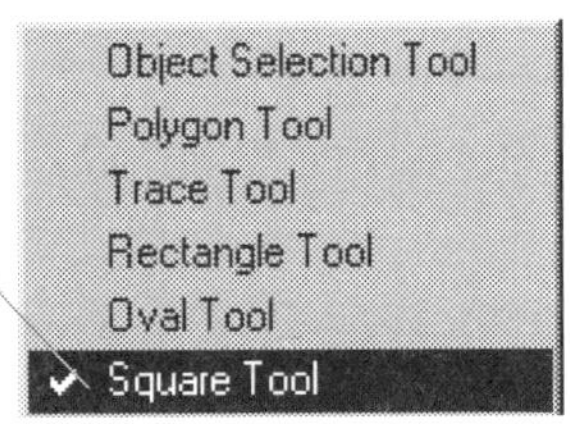

Circle

Click here and then make a circular selection on the image

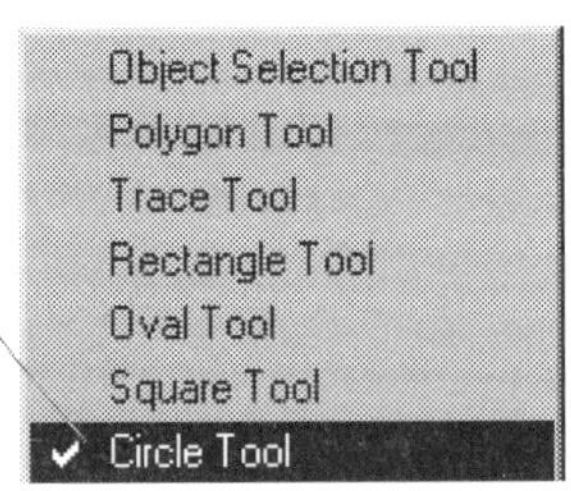

Selecting irregular objects

There are three tools that can be used to select irregularly shaped objects such as trees, people or cars. This requires a bit more care than when selecting symmetrical objects but the results are just as effective.

Making freehand selections can be a frustrating business at first. Make sure the entire object that you want to select is visible on screen and if you need to move your hand while making the selection, lift the mouse off the mouse-mat to do so. This way it will not move the cursor and affect your selection.

Trace

This can be used to make a completely freehand selection around an object. It is best for selecting a general area rather than one that needs a lot of precision.

Click here and then draw a freehand selection on the image. It can be hard to make an exact selection with this method. One alternative is to make a selection that leaves a small border around the object, which can be edited at a later date with a technique such as cloning

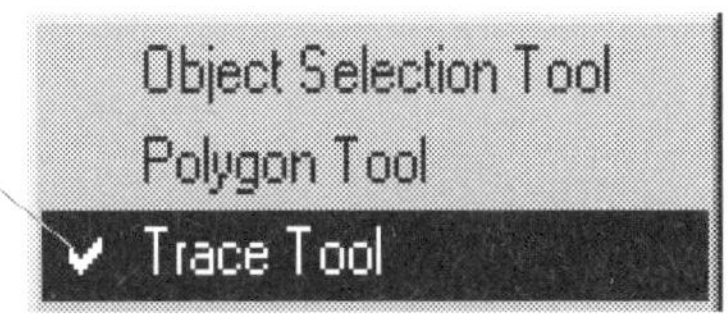

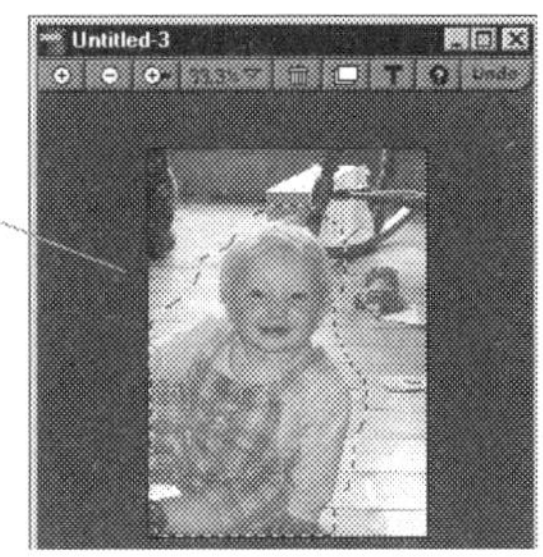

Follow steps 1-2 on page 71 to launch the menu shown here.

Polygon

This can be used in exactly the same way as the Trace tool, but it can also be used to draw straight lines around an irregularly shaped object.

Make sure your mouse is working properly when making freehand selections. If necessary, take out the rubber ball that moves on the mouse-mat and give it a good clean.

Click here and then click once on the image. Move the cursor to the point on the image where you want the line to go to and click again. Repeat this until the selection is complete

SmartSelect

The SmartSelect tool selects irregularly shaped objects by identifying colour differences along the selection path and then adjusts the selection accordingly. For instance, if a black object is being selected against a white background, the SmartSelect tool will automatically snap the selection so that it follows the border of the black object. To make a selection with the SmartSelect tool:

If you move the cursor to the wrong position it is possible to return to the last marker on the selection by retracing the line that you have most recently made.

1 Click here to select the SmartSelect tool

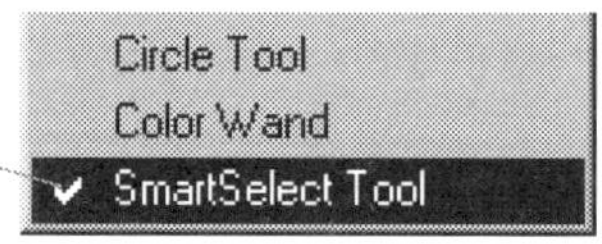

2 The SmartSelect Options dialog box appears automatically. Use the Edge Threshold box to set how sensitive the SmartSelect tool is to differences in colour. The values are between 1 and 100 pixels and the higher the setting, the more sensitive it is. Use the Brush Width box to set how close the selection has to be to the desired edge for the SmartSelect tool to work. The values are between 1 and 20 pixels and the higher the setting, the larger the area that is searched for colour differences

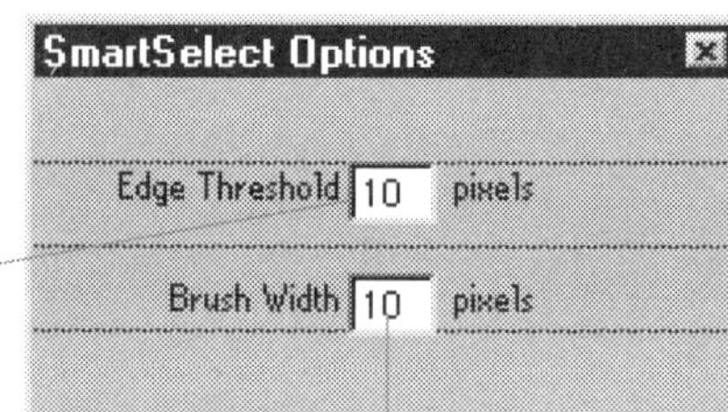

To remove an outline marker, move the cursor back over it and press Delete. This will delete all of the selection that came after the marker. This can only be done with the most recent marker that has been placed.

3 Click at the start of the selection and then start to trace around the desired area. Do not click the mouse as the SmartSelect tool will locate the edges and place markers accordingly

Color Wand tool

The Color Wand tool offers a quick way to select an area of the same, or similar, colour. Before a selection is made, the tolerance for the colour wand can be set to determine the range of colour that the tool will identify to be selected. To use the Color Wand tool:

1 Select File>Preferences>Cursors from the Advanced Menus

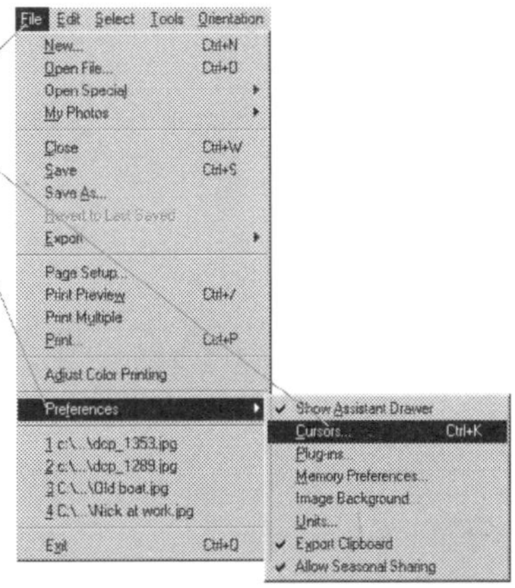

The value in the Color Wand Tolerance box also applies to the Color Change tool. This is the tool for changing coloured areas on an image and is discussed in more detail in Chapter Seven.

2 In the Cursors dialog box, enter a value in the Color Wand Tolerance box. A low value will result in only similar colours being selected, while a high value will result in a wider range of colours being selected

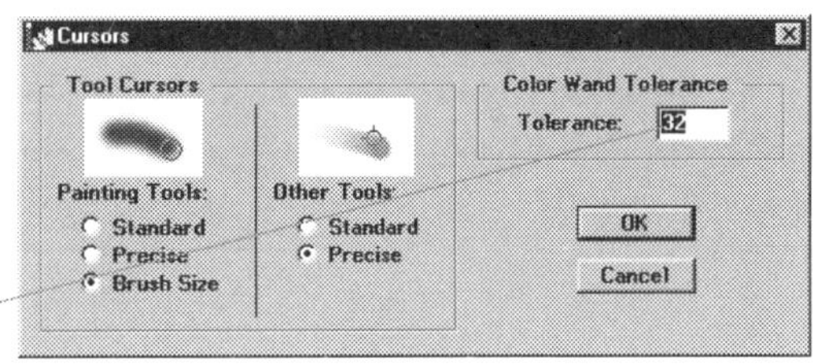

Follow steps 1-2 on page 71 to launch the menu shown here.

3 Click here in the selection menu to select the Color Wand tool

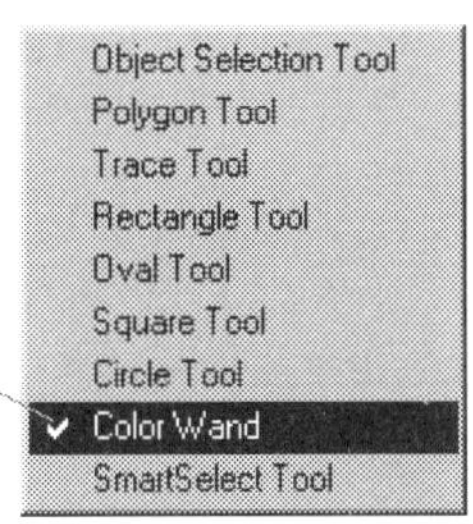

4 Click on the colour in the image that you want to select. This will apply to similar colours anywhere in the image

Once a selection has been made with the Color Wand it may have created selections in different areas of the image. For instance, if it is set to select red, and shades of red, then it would select any red objects within the image. If an editing technique is then applied, it will affect all of the selections on the image.

5 A Color Wand selection with a low level of tolerance (10 pixels). This selects colours within a very narrow range from the one that was selected on the image. This is useful for selecting solid blocks of colour within an image

6 A Color Wand selection with a high level of tolerance (80 pixels). This selects colours within a wide range of the one selected on the image. This is useful for selecting subtle colour changes such as skin tones

Resizing a selection

When using the selections tools, particularly the freehand ones, it is easy to select too much or too little of the intended area or object. Rather than having to remove the selection and start again, it is possible to retain the selected area and then add or delete another part of the image as required. To do this:

1 Make a selection on an image

Resizing is a useful way to create slightly unusual symmetrical selections such as a cross. To do this, draw a rectangle and then use the Reduce option to remove a small square from the four corners of the original shape. This technique can be used to create a variety of straight-edged selections.

2 Click here to increase the selected area

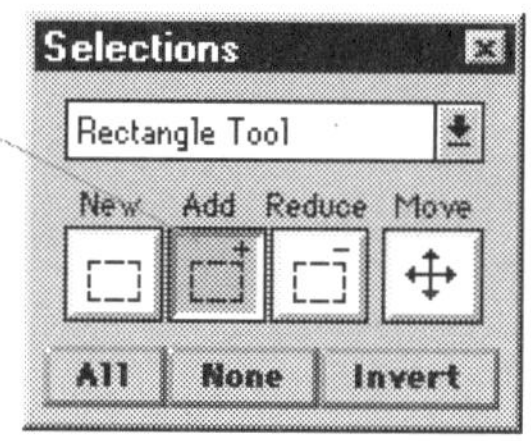

3 Select the extra part of the image that you want to include. This now becomes part of the original selection

4 Repeat the process to decrease the selected area, but click here before editing the selection

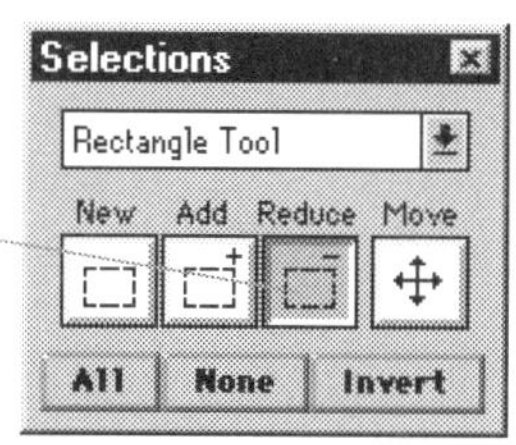

Inverting a selection

When you are selecting an object it is sometimes easier to select the area that you do not require and then invert it, so that you are left with the correct selection. This is useful in instances where you have an object such as a person or a building and you want to edit all of the image except this item. One way to do this would be to trace around the object and also the rest of the image. Alternatively, you could just select the object and then invert the selection:

If there is a symmetrical object, such as a box, that is to be left untouched while the rest of the image is selected, then it is much quicker to use the Invert method. Select the box by using the Rectangle or Square selection tools, and then select Invert.

1 Make a selection of the item that will be left untouched in the image. In this example we want to place the person against a plain white background. As the selection stands, any editing changes would apply to the person rather than the background

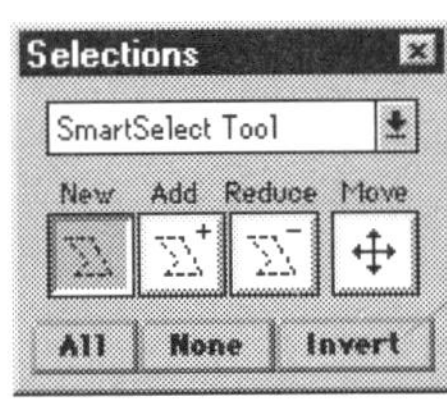

2 Select Invert from the Selections dialog box

3 The selection is now inverted so that the background is selected and the person is not

4 The background can now be edited without affecting the object that was selected originally

Filling a selection

Once a selection has been made it can filled with a different colour. This can be done with a paintbrush effect or by changing all of the similarly coloured areas in the selection:

To change the colour for the Brush and Color Change options, double-click on the colour box and then select a new colour from the Color Picker dialog box.

Filling with the Brush tool

1 Make a selection

2 Select Tools>Brush from the Advanced Menus

3 Select a brush size and colour and then fill in the selection as required by dragging the brush over it

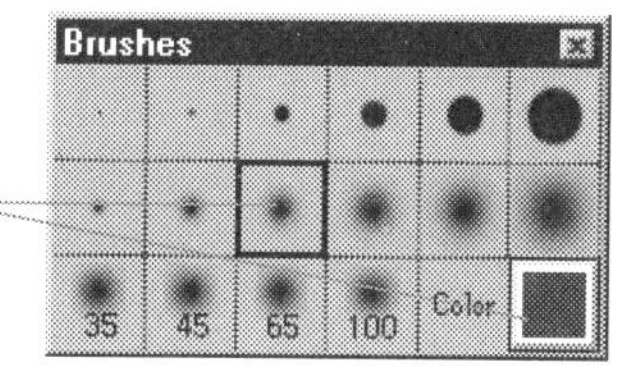

See Chapter Seven for more information about adding colour to an image.

Filling with the Color Change tool

Text cannot be added to a selection, because it is always placed on a separate layer. See Chapter Seven for more information about adding text and Chapter Six for more information about Layers.

1 Make a selection

2 Select Tools>Color Change from the Advanced Menus

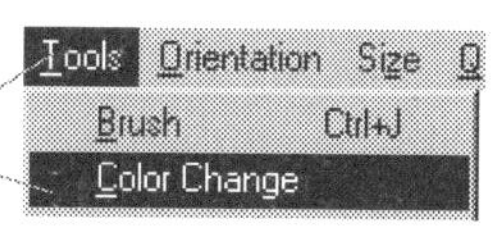

3 Click within the selection to change areas of similar colour (see Chapter Seven for more details about this technique)

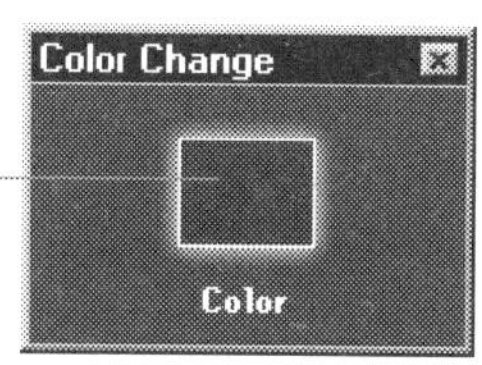

Moving a selection

Selections can be moved within the same image, or they can be copied and pasted into other images.

Moving by dragging

Moving a selection can take up a lot of computer memory. Depending on the size of your machine, you may have to drag a selection by small amounts at a time rather than moving it in one operation. This process can also cause the program to crash on occasions.

1 Make a selection

2 Select Move

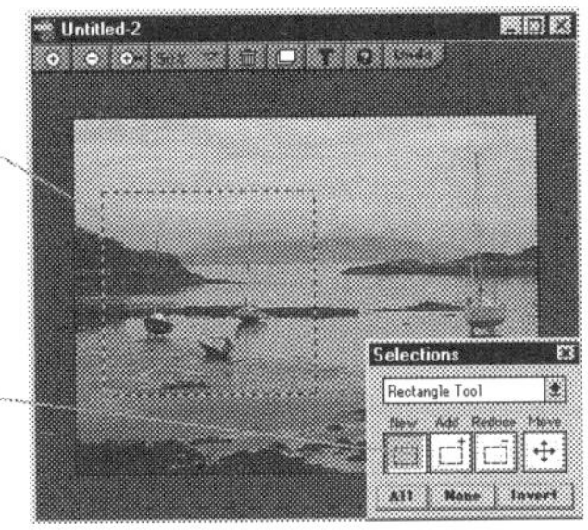

3 Place the cursor inside the selection. When it changes to a four-headed arrow, drag the selection to its new location

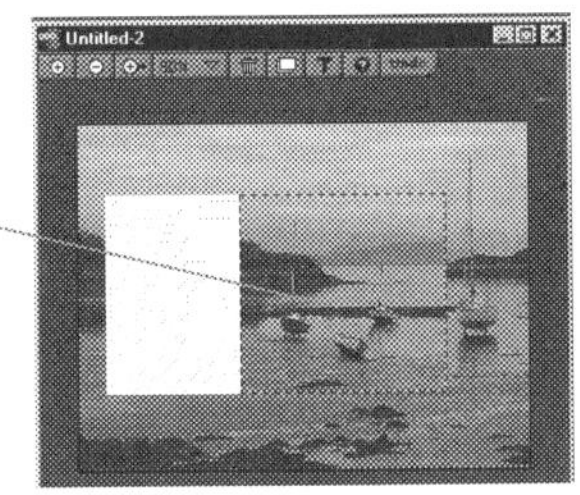

Moving by copying and pasting

1 Make a selection as above

2 Select Edit>Copy (or Cut) from the Advanced Menus

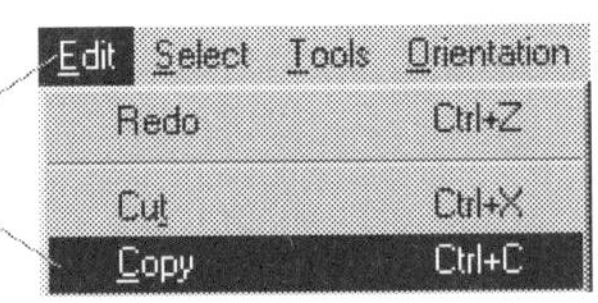

3 In the required location select Edit>Paste and then reposition by dragging if required

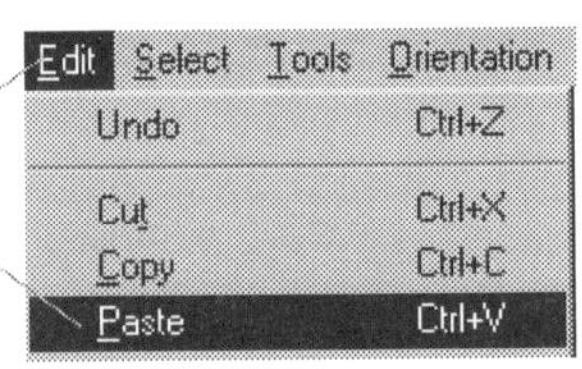

Copying and pasting between images

A selection can be copied and pasted into another image in much the same way as it would be in the same image:

Multiple images can be viewed on screen at the same time but this limits the viewing size of each of them. Also, with more images open, a greater amount of RAM will be required to process them all.

1. Open two images and display them together on the screen by selecting Window>Tile

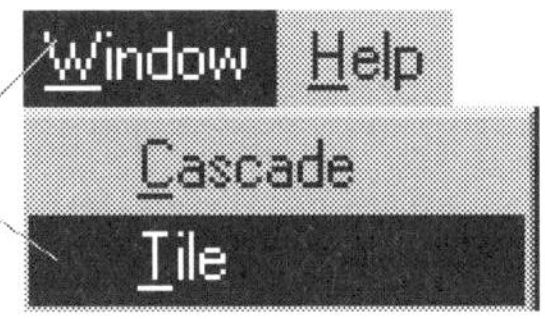

2. Make a selection on the first image

3. Select Edit>Copy

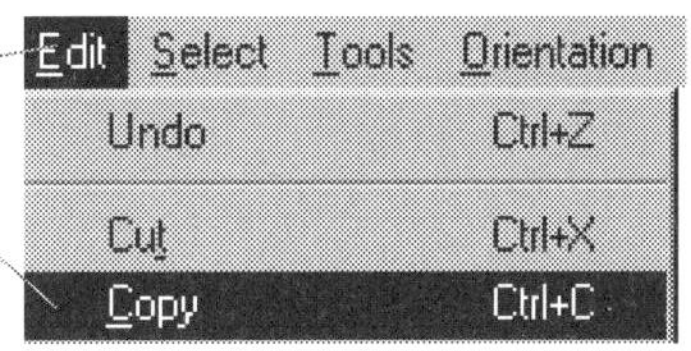

For further details on creating and using layers, see Chapter Six.

4. Select the second image and select Edit>Paste

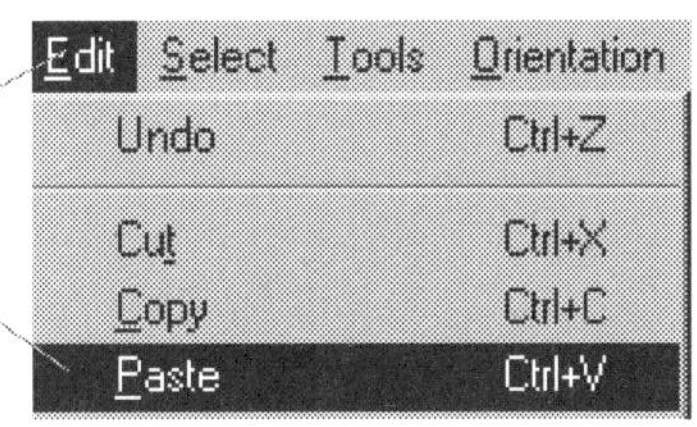

5. The selection is pasted into the second image as a new layer. This means it can be edited independently from the other items in the image

Deleting a selection

As well as being edited, selections can also be removed altogether. This may be because an object such as a telegraph pole appears to be growing out of the top of someone's head, or if you want to remove an individual from a group photograph. However, once a selection has been deleted there will be a gap in the image from where it was removed. This then requires a little work to get the image back to an acceptable condition:

A selection can also be deleted by selecting Edit>Delete from the Advanced Menus. Select Edit>Cut to remove the selection but save it to the clipboard so that it can then be pasted back somewhere else.

1. Make a selection

2. Delete the selection by pressing Delete or the Backspace key on the keyboard

3. There is now a space where the selection has been removed. Select Tools>Clone from the Advanced Menus

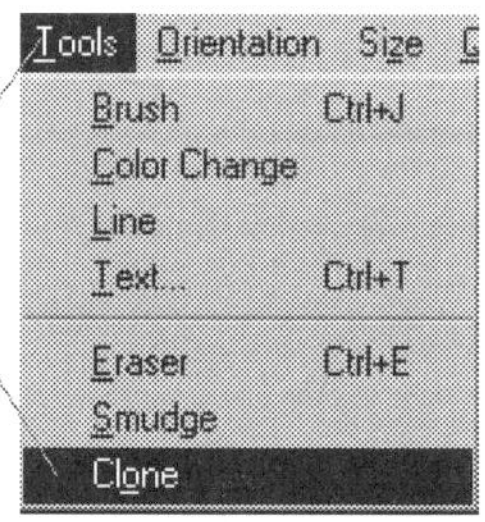

4. Select a size for the Clone tool and clone the space using the cloning technique described in Chapter Four

Working with layers

Chapter Six

This chapter looks at how complex and eye-catching images can be created by placing different elements on separate layers within the same image.

Covers

Layers defined

Layering is a PhotoDeluxe device that allows for numerous elements to be combined into a single image. This is done by placing each element on a different layer. These layers can then be accessed individually and the contents can be edited without affecting any of the other elements (on different layers) within the image. It is similar to creating an image by using several sheets of transparent film. Each sheet can have individual items on it but once all of the sheets are put together in order, a complete image appears. If you want to change a certain element in the image then you would simply remove the relevant sheet, make the necessary amendments and then replace the sheet. In PhotoDeluxe, layers can be used for a variety of reasons:

DON'T FORGET: *A single image can be made up of a maximum of 99 layers. However, this is likely to produce a very large file size that will require a lot of processing power.*

- Adding text to an image
- Adding independent paint effects
- Creating montages
- Combining graphics and photographic images

DON'T FORGET: *Text is always added to a separate layer. Each image can only have one Text layer and it is always the topmost one.*

A layered image

1 These three images are all individual layers

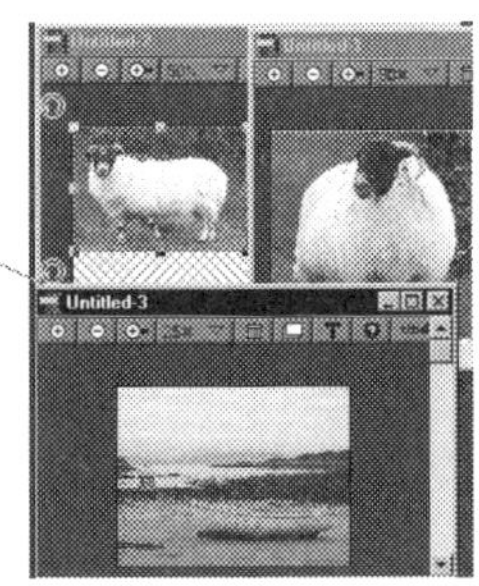

2 When viewed together they create a complete image

The Layers palette

Layers within an image are controlled with the Layers palette. This can be used to view the layers within an image, create new layers, edit existing layers and rearrange the order of layers. To view the Layers palette:

If you are working with a layered image, make sure the Layers palette is visible at all times. Otherwise you may lose track of the different elements in the image.

1 Select View>Show Layers from the Advanced Menus

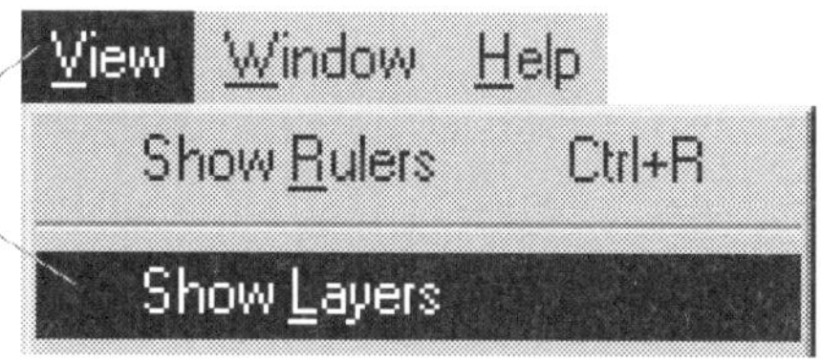

2 The Layers palette displays which layers are part of the selected image and offers a variety of editing options

It is perfectly possible to work with digital images and never use the layers options. However, they do give you an extra tool in your image editing armoury and they are a very flexible option to have available.

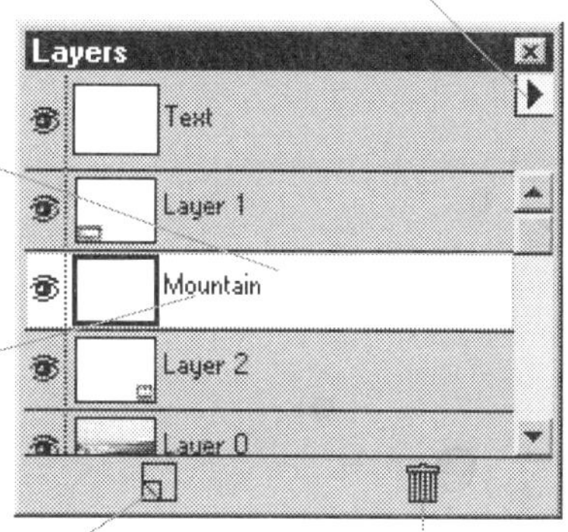

Click here to access the Layers palette menu (see below)

Each layer is shown as a thumbnail. The active layer is highlighted

Each layer can be given an individual name

Click here to create a new layer

Click here to delete a layer

The Layers palette menu, accessed via the arrow at the top right of the palette

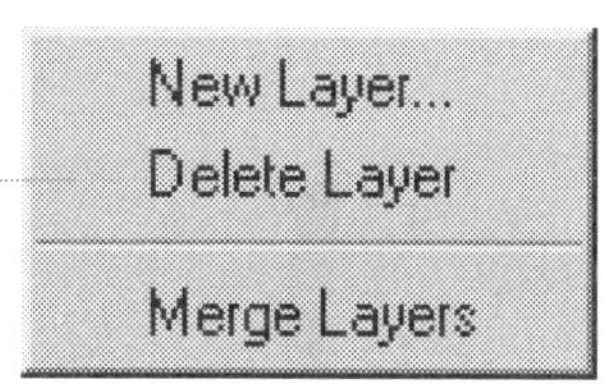

Creating a new blank layer

New layers can be created in a variety of ways, some of which create layers that are empty while others create layers that already consist of objects.

Creating a blank layer

Always give a new layer a meaningful name. This might not seem necessary when you only have two or three layers in a image, but if you have several dozen then you will want to know the exact definition for each one.

1. Make sure the Layers palette is showing (View>Show Layers from the Advanced Menus) and then click on the Create New Layer icon

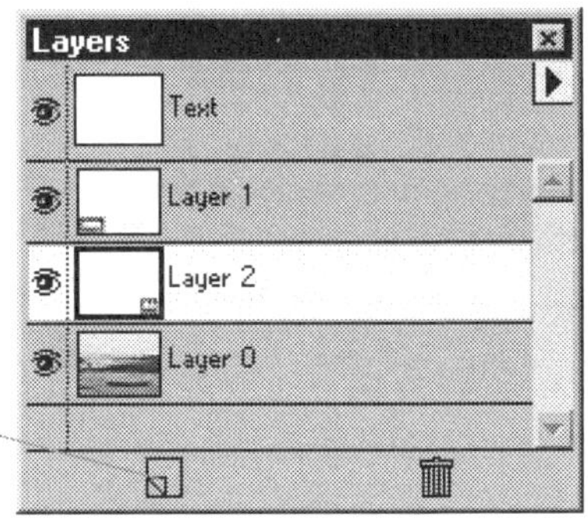

2. In the New Layer dialog box type a name for the new layer.

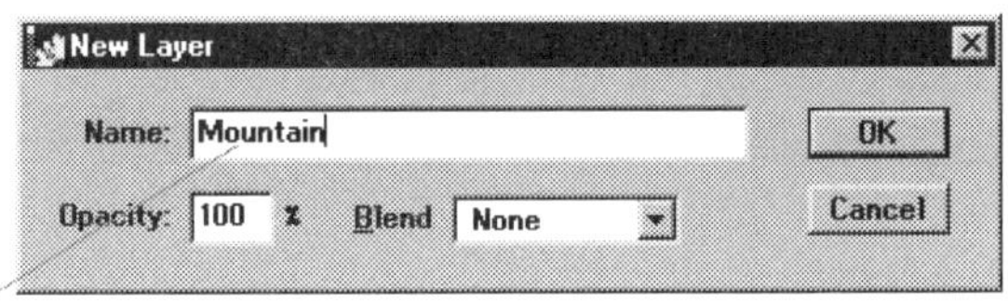

There are also options for the opacity of the layer and the Blend option. For the moment, leave these at the default settings, which means the layer will be completely transparent and not blended. Select OK

Blank layers can have content added to them after they have been created.

3. The new layer now appears in the Layers palette. It has no content and it is completely transparent

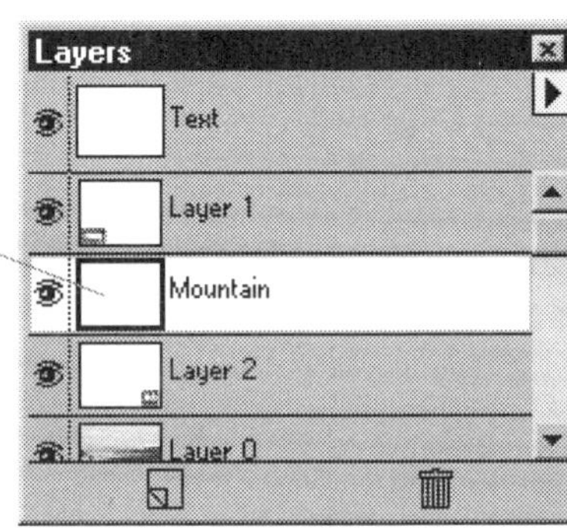

Creating layers from other images

By using layers it is possible to combine two or more complete images, or copy a selected area from one image and add it to another image as a new layer.

Creating a layer from a complete image

If a new layer is created in this way then it appears on top of the layer it has been dragged onto. To change the stacking order of layers, select the Stacking Order button on the Image toolbar.

1. Open two images and position them side-by-side by selecting Window>Tile from the Advanced Menus. Select the image where you want to create the new layer

2. Drag one image and release it on top of the other one

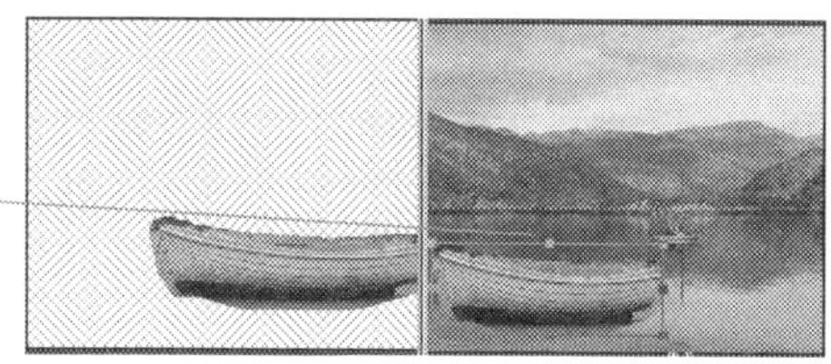

or

Drag one of the thumbnails from the Open Photo area and drop it on top of the active image

3. With both methods the image that has been dragged becomes a new layer on the other image

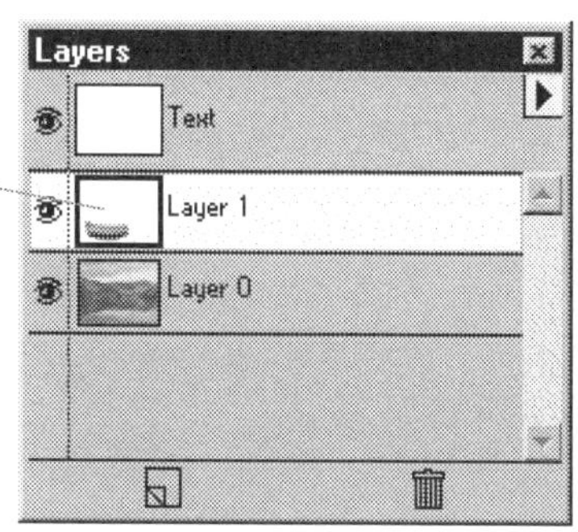

Creating a new layer using a selection

If you want to create a new layer on an image using only part of another image then this can be done by using the copy and paste commands:

1. Open two images and position them side-by-side by selecting Window>Tile from the Advanced Menus

2. Select the part of the image that you want to copy to the second image. Select Edit>Copy

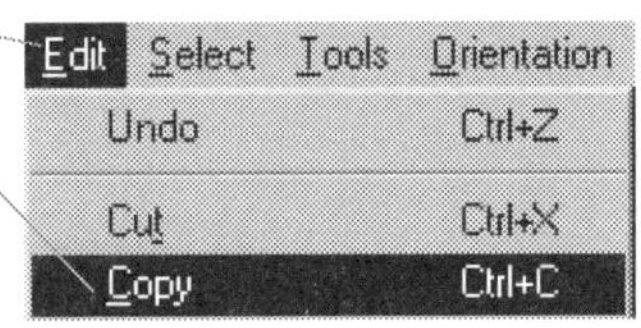

Selections can be made from numerous images and then added to a single image. Each new selection will create a new layer. However, each new layer increases the file size of the image.

3. Select the second image. Select Edit>Paste

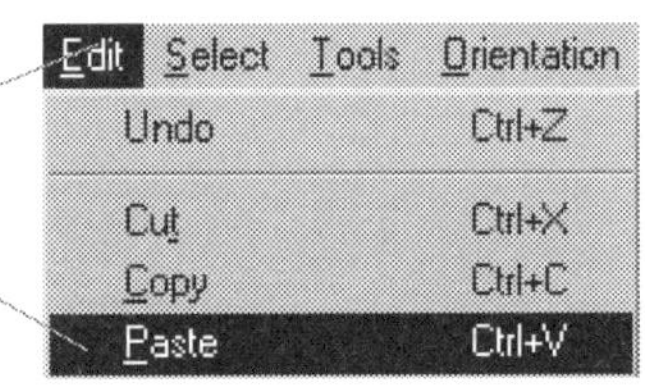

4. The selection is added to the image as a new layer

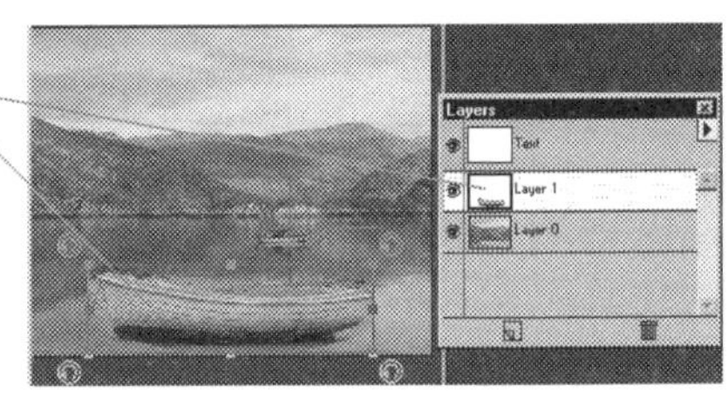

Selecting layers

Once a layer has been created it can be selected at any time so that editing changes can be made to it:

1. Locate the required layer from the Layers palette and click on it once to activate it

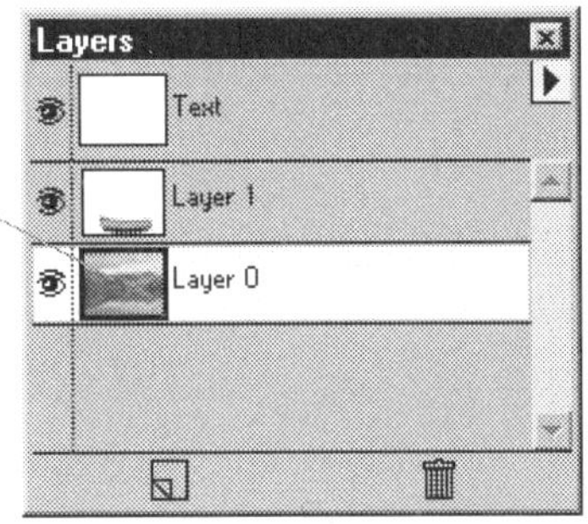

If you are trying to make an editing change to a layer and it does not appear to be working, check that you have the correct layer selected. If you have a different one selected then the editing function may not appear as expected.

2. The on-screen image will probably look the same but the active layer is the one that is being edited

3. Edit the layer. Any changes that are made will only affect this layer. If the active layer is on top of other layers then it may seem as if the editing changes are being applied to them too. However, only one layer can be edited at a time

Resizing and rotating layers

If a layer has been created from another image it may not be the right size or in the correct position for the new image. Any layer can be resized or have its orientation changed by rotating it:

To resize an image proportionally, hold down Shift when you are dragging the resizing handles.

1. Select a layer from the Layers palette by clicking on it once

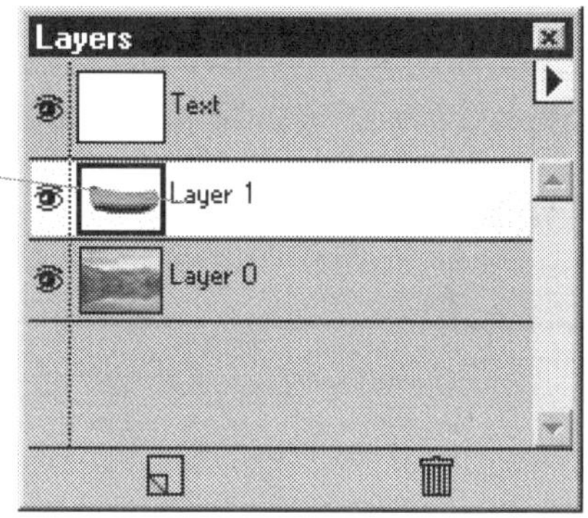

2. Alternatively, click on a layer in an image. This will activate the resizing and rotating handles

3. Drag a central handle to change the size of the layer

4. Drag a corner handle to change the layer's orientation

Deleting layers

Layers can be deleted in a similar way to which they are created:

When you are deleting a layer, always double-check that you do not require any of the elements on it any more. Once it has been deleted it can only be restored if you click Undo immediately after the layer has been removed.

1. Select a layer from the Layers palette by clicking on it once

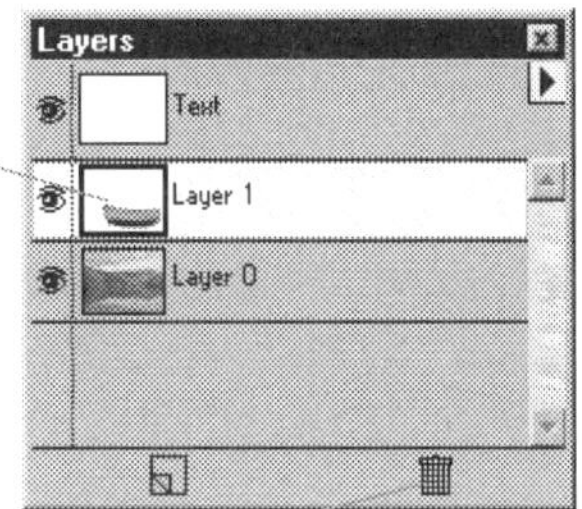

2. Click on the Wastebasket icon on the Layers palette to remove the layer

   or

   Select the layer and delete it by selecting the Wastebasket icon from the toolbar

3. The layer is removed from the Layers palette and the image

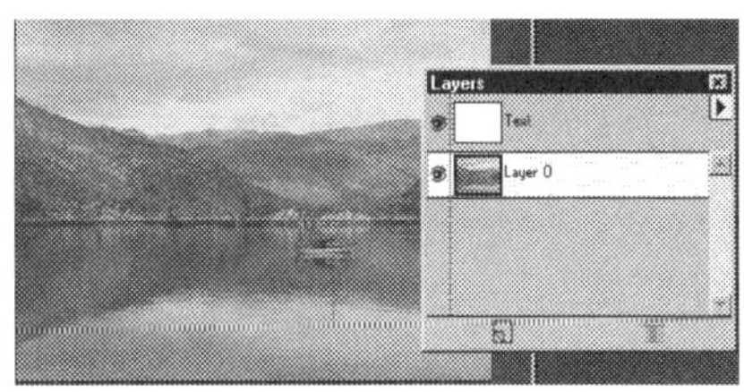

Showing and hiding layers

Any number of layers on an image can be hidden from view. This can be useful if there are a lot of layers in an image and you just want to work on one, without the others getting in the way. To show and hide layers:

If a layer has been hidden it does not mean the layer has been removed. It is still part of the image, even though it cannot be seen.

1. Make sure the Layers palette is visible (select View>Show Layers from the Advanced Menus)

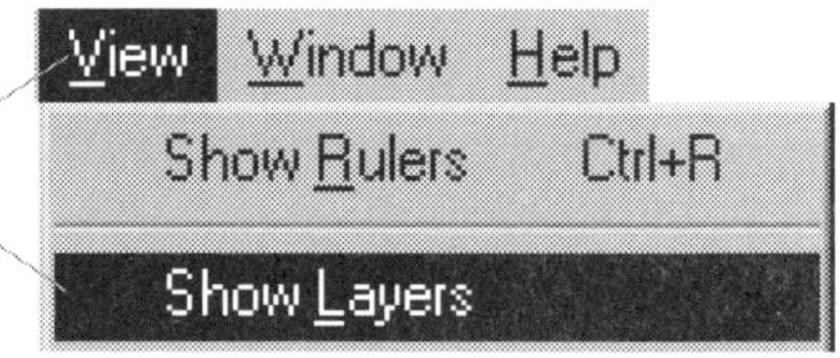

2. Click on the eye icon in the Layers palette to hide a layer. This then hides the layer on the active image

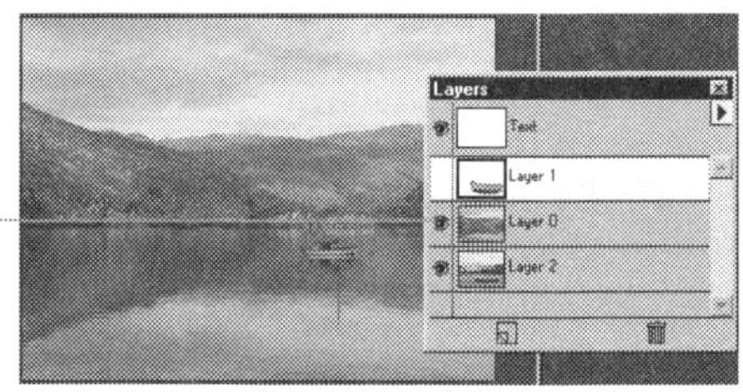

The Text layer can be hidden in the same way as any other layer in the image, by clicking on the eye icon in the Layers palette. However, it does not become hidden using the procedure in Step 4.

3. Click in the column containing the eye icon to show the layer again

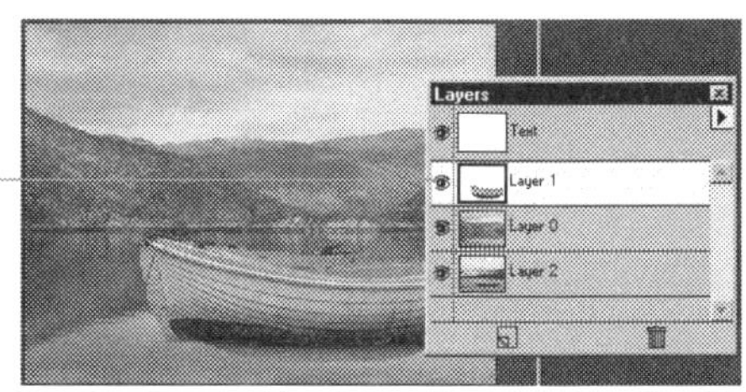

4. To hide all but one layer and the Text layer, hold down Alt and click on the layer you want to view. All of the other layers except the Text layer will be hidden

Merging layers

Each layer in an image contributes to an increase in the overall file size: 10 separate layers take up more disc space than if they were all combined into one image. It is therefore good image editing housekeeping to merge layers together whenever possible. To do this:

Only merge a layer when you are sure you have finished making any editing changes to it. Once a layer has been merged it cannot then be edited independently.

1 Hide any layers that you do not want to merge, by clicking on their eye icons in the Layers palette

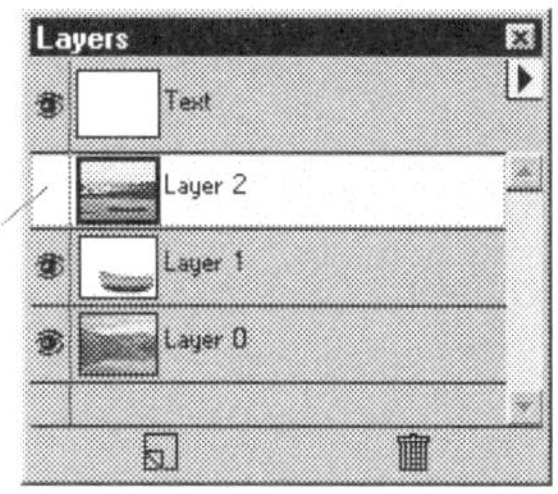

2 Select any visible layer from the Layers palette

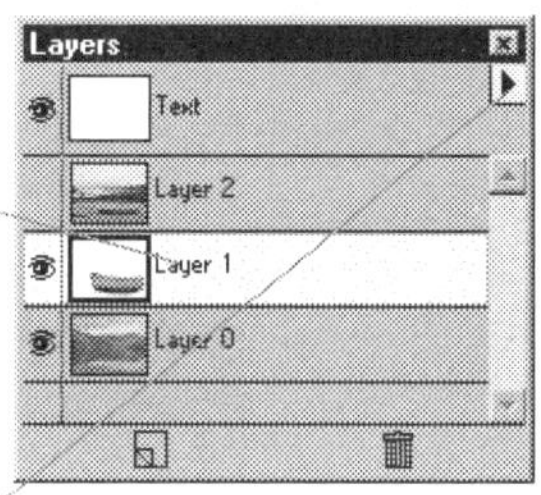

All the layers that are not hidden will be combined when the Merge command is chosen.

3 Click here to open the Layers palette menu

4 Select Merge Layers

The Text layer cannot be merged with any other layers within the image.

5 All the active layers become merged, as shown in the Layers palette

Setting opacity

The opacity of a layer determines how much of the layer immediately below can be seen through it. This can create interesting effects and it is a good way to merge different layers into one seamless image. To set the opacity:

The opacity can also be set when a new layer is created. Add the value in the Layers Option dialog box at the same time as giving a name to a new layer.

1 Double-click a layer on the Layers palette to activate the Layers Option dialog box

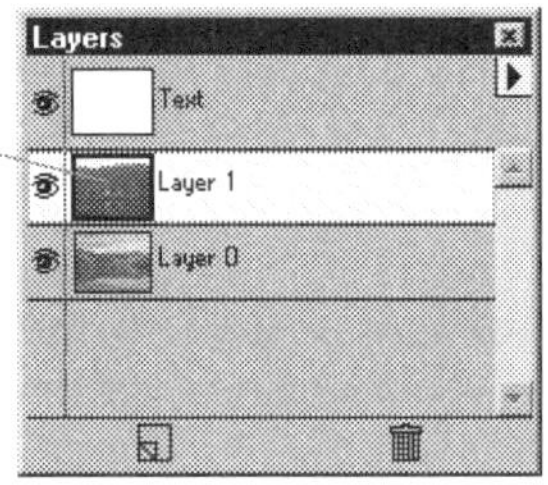

2 Enter a percentage value here for the opacity of the image

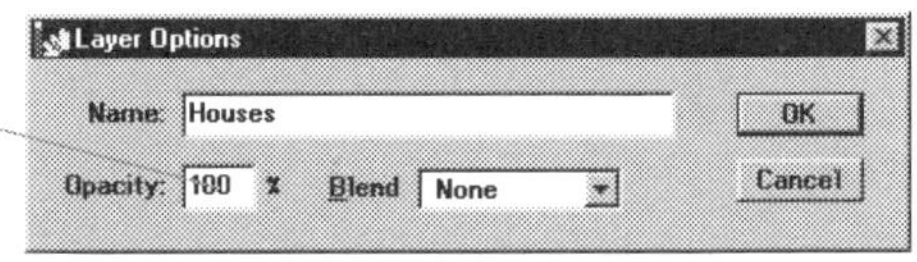

3 An opacity value of 100% means that none of the layer below can be seen

4 A lower value, such as 30%, allows for a significant amount of the layer below to be seen

Blending layers

One of the most artistic uses for layers is to blend them together using various blending modes. This combines layers and mixes the colours together, rather than just placing one layer on top of another. This can produce some striking effects, but it is a technique that requires a reasonable amount of practise. When blending colours there are three main areas to consider:

- The base colours, which are contained within the original image
- The blend colours, which are the colours being blended
- The result colours, which are the colours in the blended image

When using blend modes it is advantageous to have some knowledge of how different colours interact with each other. However, if you do not, it can be fun experimenting to see what kinds of effects can be achieved.

Setting a blend mode

There are five methods for blending layers and these can be selected when a layer is created or at any point thereafter. To set the blend mode:

1. Double-click a Layer on the Layers palette to activate the Layers Option dialog box

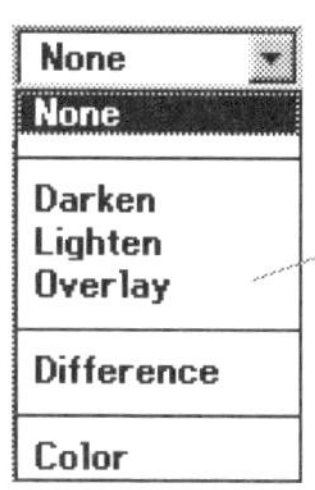

2. Click here to activate the blend menu

Darken blending

This selects the darkest colours in two images and uses these to create the result colour.

Using the Darken blend a light image is blended with a dark background to produce an atmospheric image

Use blends together with opacity for even more effective results.

Lighten blending

This selects the lightest colours in two images and uses these to create the result colour.

Blends do not always create crystal clear images and this is not the intention. Instead, they can be used to achieve artistic effects.

Using the Lighten blend a dark image is blended with a light background to produce a bright image

Overlay blending

This largely retains the colours from both images

Using the Overlay blend creates an effect that is an accurate blend of the two images (very little colour information is discarded)

The Difference mode can create similar effects to those seen in pop-art posters, where the colours are deliberately distorted and exaggerated for effect.

Difference blending

This blends two images by combining the red, green and blue colour values in each image. This can produce some interesting abstract effects.

Color blending

This creates a result colour using the lightness value of the base colour and the hue and saturation of the blend colour. This means that the base colour stays the same and the blend colour changes. This can be useful if the base image is black and white and you want to blend it with a coloured image.

Arranging layers

If you want to rearrange the way that objects appear in an image, this can be done by changing the stacking order of the layers. This alters the order in which they are viewed. For instance, the bottom layer could be moved to the top, so that all of this content would be visible and may cover some of the layers below, depending on what it contains. To change the stacking order of layers:

Note that the options for changing the stacking order of a layer are:

- *Send to Back, which puts the layer at the very bottom of the stacking order*
- *Send Back One, which puts the layer behind the immediately preceding layer*
- *Bring Forward One, which moves the layer in front of the layer above it*
- *Bring to Front, which moves the layer to the top of the stacking order (apart from the Text layer)*

1. Select a layer on an image or in the Layers palette

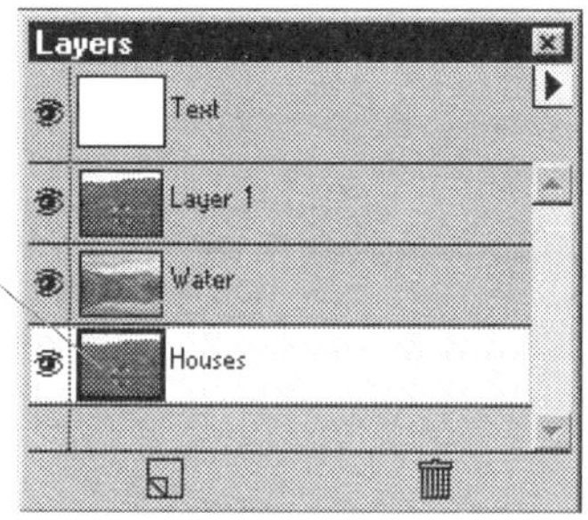

2. Click here for the stacking order options

3. Once the stacking order has been changed, the layer occupies its new position in the image and this is reflected by its position in the Layers palette

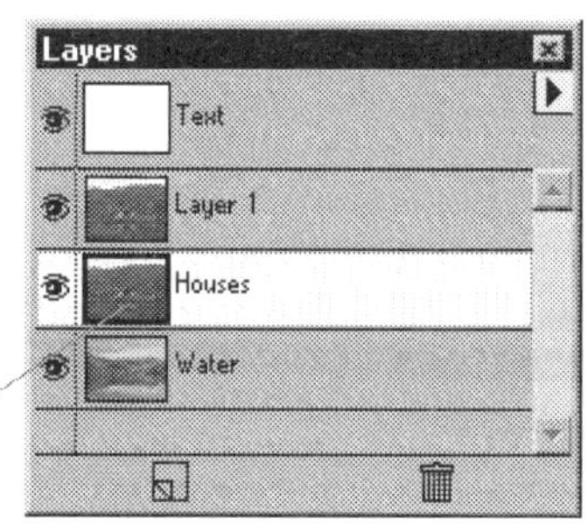

Text always resides on the top layer and this cannot be altered. If you try and change the stacking order of a Text layer, nothing will happen.

Adding text and colour

Adding additional elements to images can enhance them greatly in terms of presentation and the information they contain. This chapter examines how text and colour can be added to images and shows some of the effects that can be achieved.

Covers

Chapter Seven

Uses for text

Although PhotoDeluxe is an image editing program, it also allows for text to be inserted into images. This can be put to a number of uses:

- Creating a postcard style image

Images taken with a digital camera can be viewed instantly via a LCD panel at the back of the camera. This makes them ideal for workers who are working away from their office — problem areas such as broken equipment can be captured on a digital camera and the image can then be emailed to a central location for analysis.

- Creating your own celebratory greeting, such as for a birthday or an anniversary
- Adding explanatory notes to an image e.g. 'The new baby weighed 8 lbs and has blue eyes'
- Identifying a particular element for an architect who is working remotely from where the building is being constructed e.g. 'Here is the door that seems to open the wrong way'
- Providing textual evidence to add to an image for an insurance claim, such as a car accident or an accident in the home

Inserting text

Text can be inserted into any image and then moved or edited as required. Text is added using a new layer. Each image can only have one Text layer and it is always the top layer in the image. However, several textual elements can be added to the Text layer. To add text to an image:

*If an image that has had text added to it is saved in a proprietary file format (with the extension *.pdd or *.pbd) then it will still be possible to edit the text once the file has been closed and then reopened. However, if the file is saved in another format (such as TIFF or a JPEG), then the Text layer will be merged with the other layers and so be unavailable for editing.*

1 Open an image and select the Text icon

3 Type the text here

2 Select the font, size and text colour

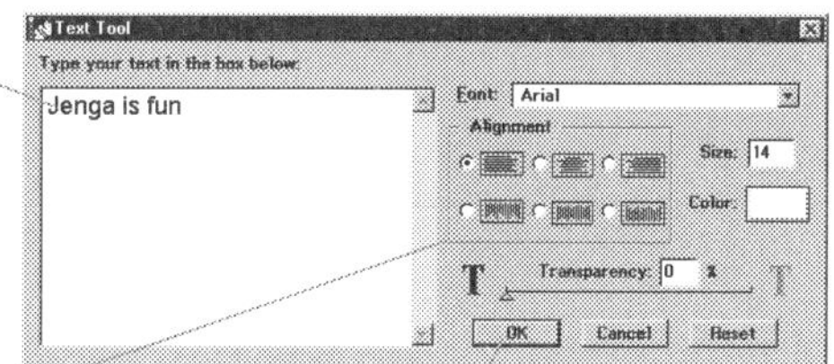

4 Select OK

To add more text to an image, repeat steps 1–4. This adds new text boxes which are independent elements, even though they are all in the same layer as other text boxes. To do this, make sure the initial text box is unselected.

5 The text appears in a text box and as a new layer in the Layers palette

Editing text

Text can be edited as follows:

1 Double-click on the text to begin editing

2 Change the font, size and colour

3 Select left, centre or right alignment

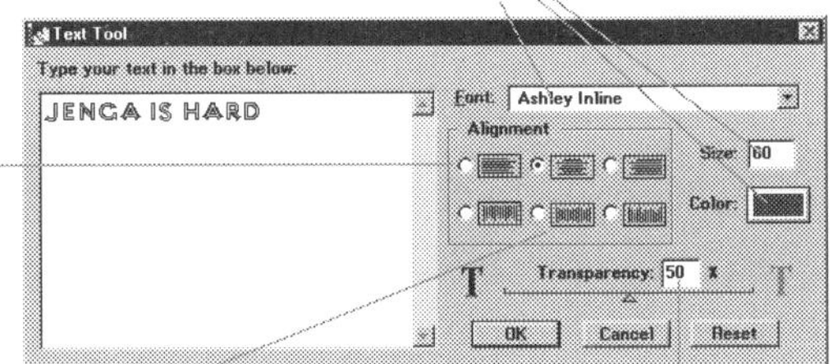

4 Click on one of these options to align the text vertically. The text can be anchored at the top, middle or bottom of the text box

5 Select a level for the transparency of the text. This determines how much of the background shows through

6 This can produce some interesting effects for the edited text

Be careful when aligning text vertically. It is not normal for the eye to read like this and it can become tiring if there is a lot of text in this format. Save this for short items such as banner headlines.

Setting a high transparency level is a useful way of creating a watermark effect with text.

Positioning text

Text can either be moved around an image by dragging it from one location to another, or it can be set at a different angle:

When text is being dragged within an image it can take up a lot of memory on the computer. It is best to try and move the text a little at a time.

Dragging text

1. Select the text and click once within the text box. Hold down the mouse button

2. Drag the text box to its new location and release

Rotated text should be used as a special effect. Do not use it as a standard formatting option.

Rotating text

1. Select the text and click once on one of the rotating handles. Keep the mouse button held down

The rotate function can also be accessed through the Advanced Menus by selecting Orientation>Free Rotate.

2. Rotate the text until the desired angle is achieved, then release

Resizing text

Text can be resized by double-clicking on the text box and then entering a new value in the text size box, as shown on page 102. This changes the point size of the text but the physical size of the text can also be altered by dragging the handles on the text box. To do this:

1 To stretch the text horizontally, click and drag these resizing handles

If text is stretched horizontally or vertically it can appear distorted. If this is the intention then it can be a useful effect.

2 To stretch the text vertically, click and drag these resizing handles

3 To stretch the text vertically and horizontally, click and drag these resizing handles

4 To stretch the text proportionally, hold down Shift and click and drag the resizing handles in Step 3

Text stacking order

Numerous text boxes can be added to the Text layer. In the majority of cases, each text box occupies its own area on the image. However, it is possible to overlap text boxes, with the last one to be included appearing on top of any others. This can be used to create effects such as shadow text and it is possible to change the order in which each text box appears on the image. To do this:

1 Select a text box and then click on the Change Stacking Order button

If there are too many overlapping text boxes on an image there is a danger that the one on the top will obscure parts of the ones below it.

2 Choose an option:

- Sends the text to the back of the Text layer
- Sends the text box behind the next closest one in the Text layer
- Brings the text box in front of the next closest one in the Text layer
- Brings the text to the front of the Text layer

3 The text boxes can then be arranged as desired

Paint basics

PhotoDeluxe has a number of functions that are similar to painting on a traditional canvas. These include:

- Changing the background colour of an image
- Filling selections with colour
- Using brushstrokes to added coloured elements to an image
- Drawing coloured lines
- Smudging and merging colours to give a smoother appearance

You do not have to have any great artistic talent to add coloured elements to an image in PhotoDeluxe. However, make sure that any paint elements add something to the image, rather than just being a conspicuous blob of colour.

Each of these techniques is achieved by selecting a colour and then using a specific tool with which to apply it. This can add an extra dimension to an image:

Using the Color Picker

The Color Picker is a colour palette that determines what colour is going to be used by a particular technique. For instance, if you want to draw black lines on an image then the relevant colour must be selected in the Color Picker before the effect is employed. Foreground and Background colours can be chosen within the Color Picker. These do not apply to the foreground or background of the image but are used for different PhotoDeluxe techniques:

Once the colours have been selected for the Foreground and Background, these will be used when applying the relevant painting technique.

- Foreground is used for techniques such as brushstrokes, lines and fill colours
- Background is used for special effect techniques such as Bas-relief and Chalk and Charcoal

Setting Foreground and Background colours

1 From the Advanced Menus, select Effects> Choose Colors

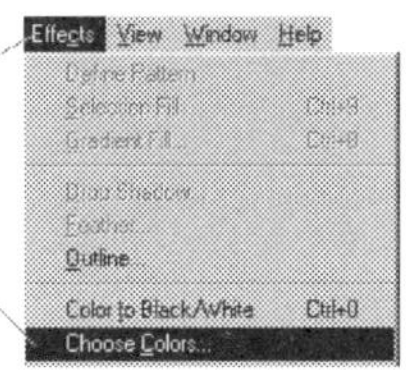

Shades of grey can also be assigned to the Foreground and Background by selecting the Greyscale palette at the bottom of the Color Picker dialog box.

2 In the Color Picker dialog box select Foreground and select a colour from the colour swatch. Repeat this for Background

All of the colour items in PhotoDeluxe, such as the Color Picker, use the American spelling. This will be followed here (and elsewhere) for the specific function, but otherwise the British spelling will be used.

3 More colours can be chosen for the Foreground and Background from this part of the Color Picker. A colour can also be selected from an open image by clicking on a colour within the image while the Color Picker is active

Brush tool

When adding brushstrokes of colour to an image, create a new layer on which to do so. This way, if you do not like the effect it can be removed by deleting the layer. If you paint the brushstrokes directly onto the image they can only be removed without affecting the rest of the image if you select Undo immediately after they have been created,

To change the brush colour, double-click on the colour button at the bottom right of the Brush palette. This will activate the Color Picker dialog box and a new colour can be selected from the colour swatches there.

The Brush tool enables brushstrokes of colour to be applied to an image. To do this:

1 Select Tools>Brush

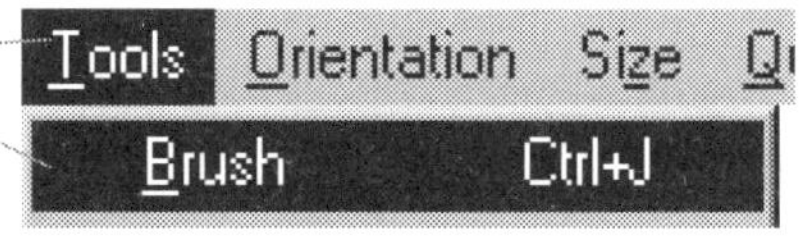

2 Select a brush size from the Brush palette (this opens automatically when the Brush option is selected)

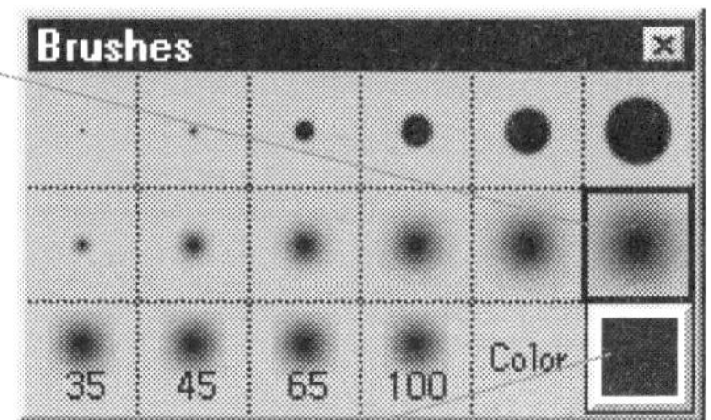

3 The colour for your brushstrokes will be shown here in the Brush palette. This will be the Foreground colour that was selected in the procedure on page 107

4 The brush is denoted by a small circle on the image. Drag this over the image to add your brushstrokes

Color Change tool

The Color Change tool enables areas of similar colours to be changed to a different colour. This can be applied within an entire image or to a selected part of an image.

Color Change within an entire image

When the Color Change tool is used it adds a solid block of colour over the area to which it is applied. If you want to recolour a variety of shades then you will have to change the Foreground colour for each differently coloured area, or change the opacity for each shade (see page 115).

1 With an image open select Tools>Color Change from the Advanced Menus

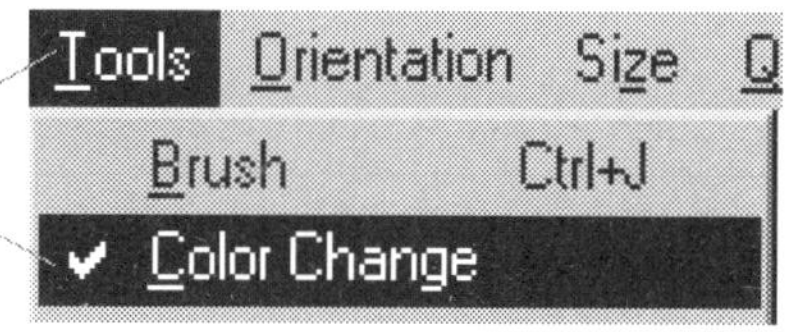

2 The Color Change box will appear, displaying the current Foreground colour. If you do not want to use this, double-click on the box. This will activate the Color Picker dialog box

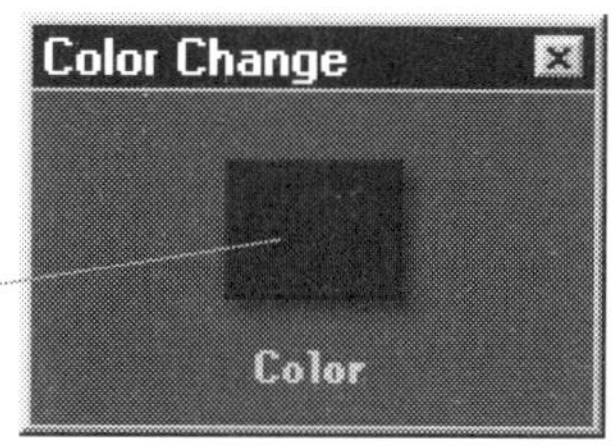

3 Select a new colour for the Color Change tool from the colour swatch. Select OK

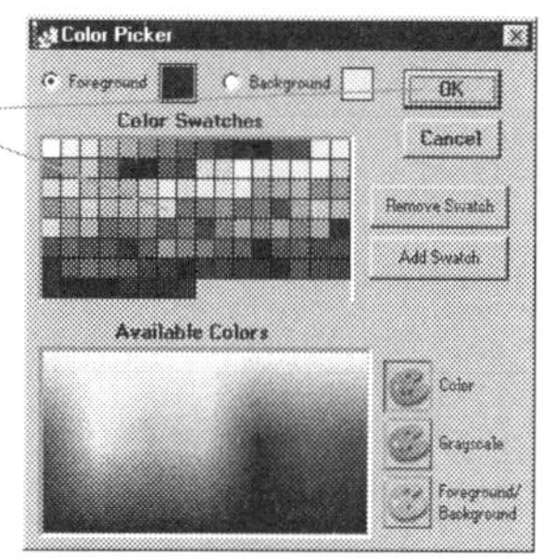

4 Position the crosshair icon on the colour that you want to change. Click once to change the colour

Using the Color Change tool on a selection

1 Select View>Show Selections from the Advanced Menus

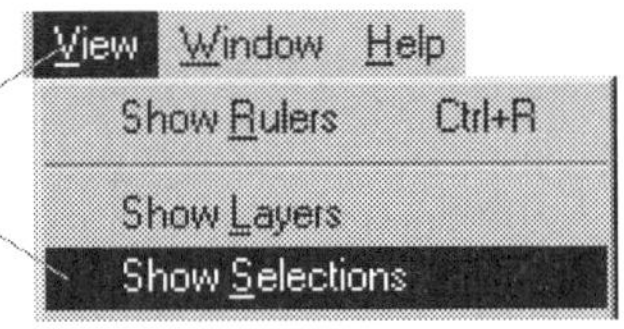

For more details about selecting objects, see Chapter Five.

2 Choose a selection tool from the Selections menu

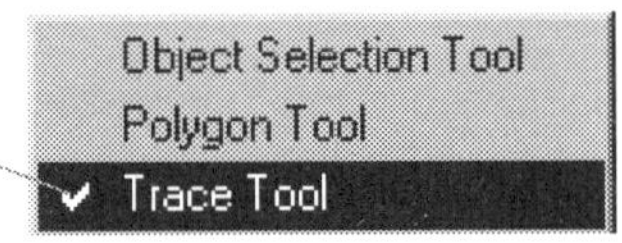

3 Select the area of the image to which you want to apply the change of colour

Once an area of an image has been selected, the Color Change tool will only work within the selection. If you try and apply it outwith the selection, nothing will happen.

4 Select Tools>Color Change from the Advanced Menus

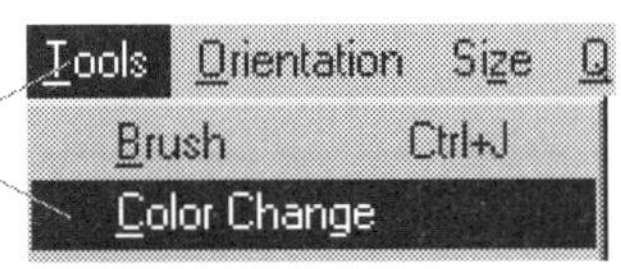

5 Use the colour in the Color Change box or select a new colour from the Color Picker dialog box

The range of colour affected by the Color Change tool will depend on the preference settings for cursors. To access this, select File>Preferences> Cursors from the Menu bar. For more information on this, see page 116

6 Position the crosshair icon within the selection and click once to recolour it

Line tool

Lines can be added to images in a variety of sizes and colours:

1 With an image open, select Tools>Line from the Advanced Menus

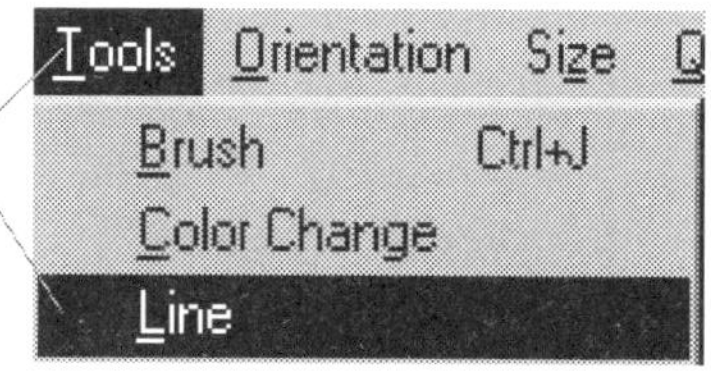

2 Set the width of the line by double-clicking here and entering a number as required (the width is measured in pixels and ranges from 1 to 1000)

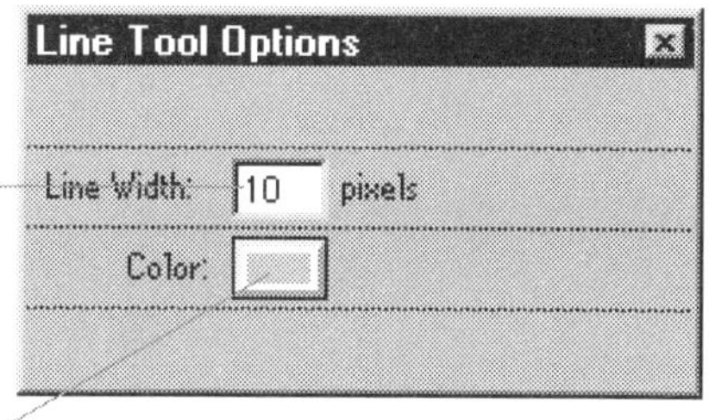

If you select a very high value for the width of a line, the result will look more like a coloured box than a line.

3 Use the colour that is already showing or double-click on it to change it in the Color Picker dialog box

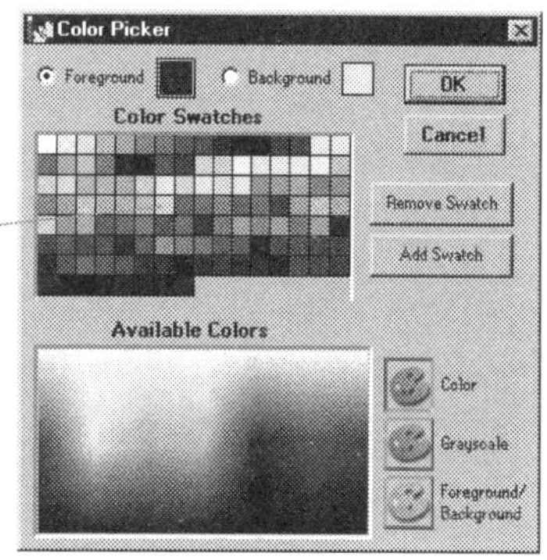

Lines are added onto the layer on which they are applied, rather than created on a new layer.

4 Click and drag to draw lines with the attributes that have been specified in Steps 2 and 3

Smudge tool

The Smudge tool produces a similar effect to the physical activity of merging paint or pastels together by rubbing them with a finger. In PhotoDeluxe this is a good way to merge adjoining colours together or to create the impression of speed by smudging the outline of a vehicle such as a car or a train. To use the Smudge tool:

The Smudge tool is effective for creating smooth skin tones and it can be used after cloning has taken place.

1 Open an image and select Tools>Smudge from the Advanced Menus

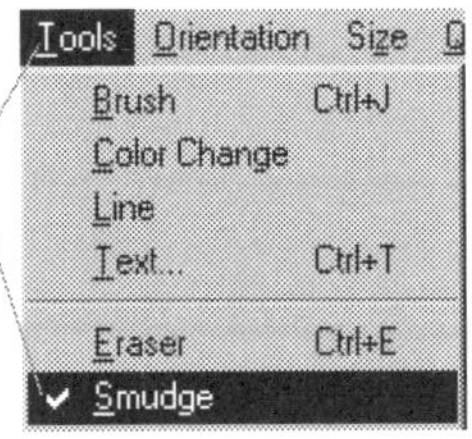

2 Select a size for the Smudge tool from the Smudges box

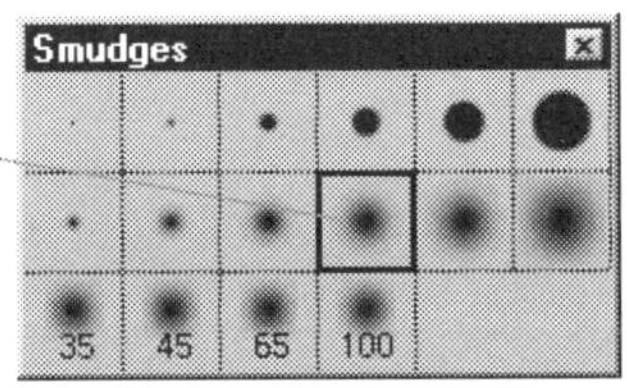

3 Smudge the image by dragging the Smudge tool over the relevant area

When selecting the strength for the smudge effect, press a number on the keyboard before you start dragging the Smudge tool.

4 Use the keyboard numbers to set the smudge strength:

- 1 for the lowest amount
- 5 for a medium amount
- 0 for the highest amount

Eraser tool

As with most creative processes, there will be times when you want to remove an element, or elements, from an image. This is done with the Eraser tool, which is similar to a rubber eraser that is used to remove pencils marks. The Eraser tool can be used on a single layer or an entire image and for both the process is the same:

The Eraser tool cannot be used to remove text. This has to be done by selecting it in the Text layer and then editing or deleting it.

1 Open an image and select Tools> Eraser from the Advanced Menus

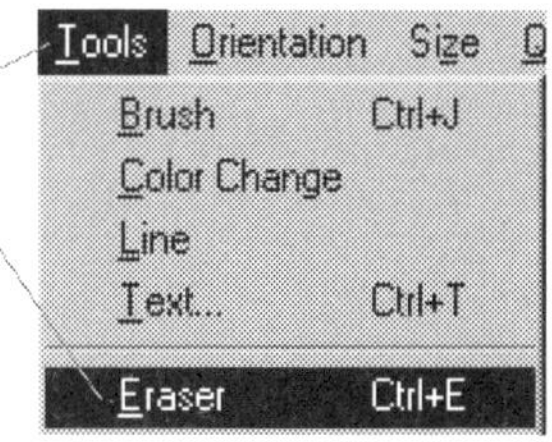

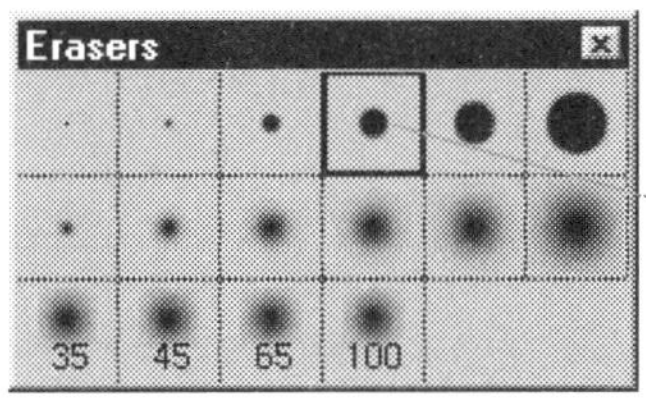

2 Select a size for the Eraser tool from the Erasers box

As with the Smudge tool, the Eraser tool can be set at various levels of strength: 1 being the weakest, 5 being medium and 0 being the strongest.

Erasing part of a layer

Elements of an individual layer can be erased, without affecting the rest of the image:

When part of a layer is erased the corresponding part of the layer immediately below it will be visible.

Select the relevant layer and then apply the Eraser tool to the part you want to remove

Erasing part of an entire image

If an image only has a single layer, or the layers have been merged together, the image background appears underneath anything that has been erased:

Apply the Eraser tool to the image. This deletes everything and leaves the background showing

The image background also appears if you change the size of the canvas. This is the area on which you view your images and it can be enlarged or reduced by selecting Size> Canvas Size from the Advanced Menu bar. This does not affect the size of the current active image.

Setting the background

If you are erasing items on the bottom layer of an image, the background will show through. By default, this is white, which usually causes no problem, unless parts of the image are white. If this is the case, then it may be difficult to tell where the image finishes and the background begins. To overcome this, it is possible to give the background a grid appearance so you can tell exactly where it is. To do this:

1. Select File> Preferences>Image Background from the Menu bar
2. Select options for the way you want the background to appear if it shows through an image

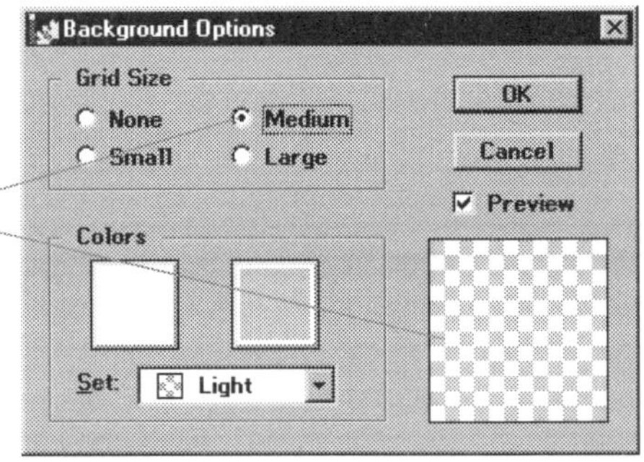

Opacity and tolerance

When adding colours to an image it is possible to specify the opacity and tolerance. The opacity is the amount of the background that shows through the added colour and the tolerance is the amount of variation of colour that is affected when a colour change is made.

Opacity can be applied to entire layers as well as areas of colours. For more information on layers, see Chapter Six.

Setting opacity

Opacity applies to drawing and painting tools, such as the Brush, Color Change and Line tools and it can be set by:

1. Select the painting option, such as Color Change, in the normal way

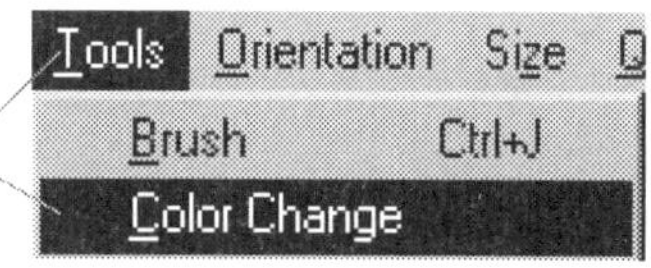

2. Before the effect is applied, press a number between 0–9 on the keyboard. This sets the level of opacity for the colour used in the selected effect:

When setting the opacity, the number on the keyboard only has to be pressed once. It does not have to be held down after it has been pressed. This level of opacity is applied to all painting tools until another level is selected.

- 1 sets the opacity at 10% which is nearly transparent;
- 5 sets the opacity at 50%;
- 0 sets the opacity at 100% which is completely solid

Setting tolerance

The tolerance determines the range of colours that are affected when either the Color Wand or the Color Change tools are used. A low tolerance value means that only very similar colours are affected; a high value means that a larger variation of colours are affected. To set the tolerance:

1. Select File>Preferences>Cursors from the Advanced Menus

2. Add a value in the Color Wand Tolerance>Tolerance box. (This applies to both the Color Wand and the Color Change tools.) Select OK

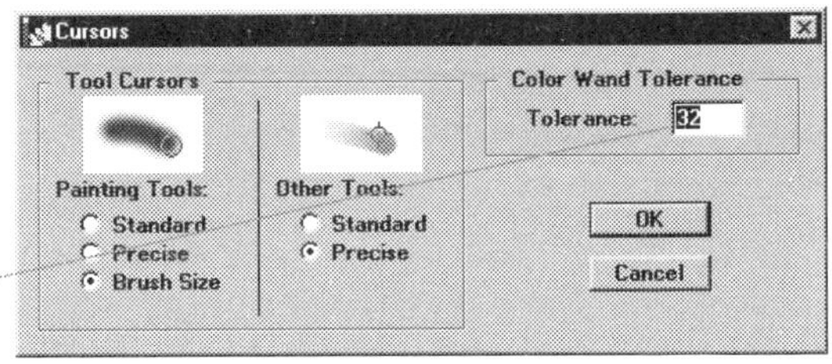

To see a clearer view of the variations in adjoining colours, view the relevant area of the image at a high magnification setting, such as 800%.

3. A low value affects a smaller range of colours

4. A high value affects a wider range of colours

Special effects

Chapter Eight

This chapter looks at some of the effects that can be applied to images using PhotoDeluxe. These range from the subtle and artistic to the outrageous.

Covers

About special effects

When you see your first digital image on a computer the thrill of this will be considerable and you may think that this is the pinnacle of your digital imaging career. However, with time you may want to extend your boundaries and let your creative instincts loose on your images. This is where the special effect features of PhotoDeluxe come into play. There is a wide range of effects that can be applied to images. Some of these are simply giving them different textures or colour effects, while others can be used to create collages or interesting lighting effects:

Each of the special effects on the Get & Fix Photo toolbar has its own step-by-step process that tells you what the effect is and then guides you through creating it.

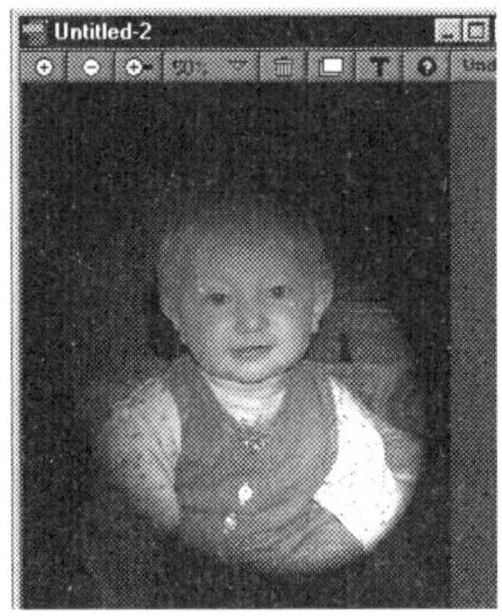

Special effects can also be selected from the Effects menu on the Advanced Menu bar. This contains similar effects to the ones on the Get & Fix Photo toolbar but they do not have the same step-by-step process and this can be quicker if you know what effect you are trying to achieve.

To access the Special Effects menus:

1 Select Get & Fix Photo>Special Effects

The first effect on the Special Effects sub-menu is for text effects. This is the same as for adding text, as described in Chapter Six.

2 Select the type of effect that you want to use and then select a specific element from its sub-menu

Artistic

These effects can be used to create similar effects to those used by an artist using either paints or pastels. Each of the effects can be created using a procedure similar to the one below, which is the Posterize effect:

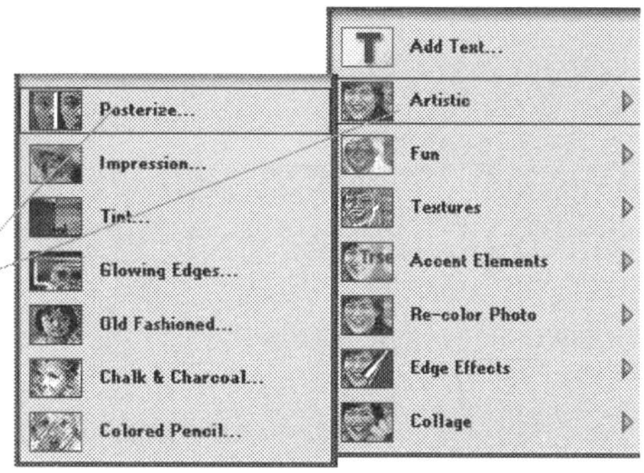

1. Select the required special effect

2. Check that the description is what you want. Click the first tab to begin creating the effect

3. Click on this box to access a dialog box for the effect

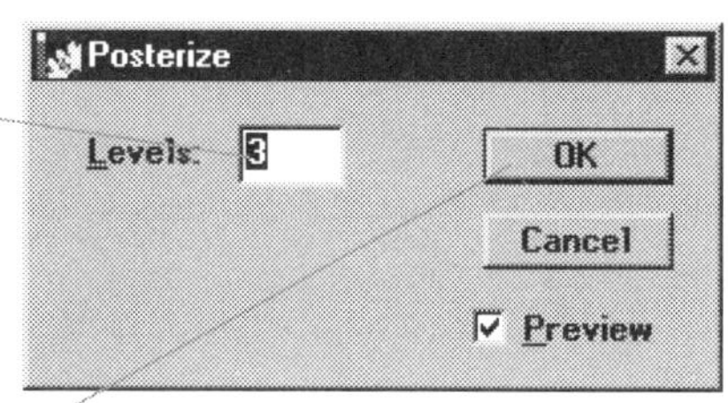

4. Enter values in the dialog box. This can alter the level at which the effect is applied. Each effect will have its own dialog box. Select OK and then the Done tab to apply the effect

Experiment with the values that you enter in the dialog boxes for the effects. If you do not like a particular result, click on the Undo button and then try some different values. There is no such thing as right or wrong when you are dealing with special effects.

Impression

This creates the effect of an Impressionist painting:

Coloured images can be quickly converted to black and white by selecting Effects>Color to Black/White from the Advanced Menu bar.

Tint

This allows you to change the colour tint of all, or part, of an image:

Some artistic special effects look better on a computer monitor than when they are printed out.

Glowing Edges

This creates a neon effect around the edges in an image:

Old Fashioned

This creates a sepia tint, like an old photograph:

Applying small values in the dialog boxes for artistic special effects usually achieves the best results. If you try and make the effect look too pronounced by applying large values, then you may end up with something that looks unnatural or unrecognisable.

Chalk & Charcoal

This creates the effect of an image drawn with pastel crayons:

As with other effects that use two colours, the Chalk & Charcoal effect combines the selected Background and Foreground colour to create the effect.

Colored Pencil

This mimics an image drawn with coloured pencils:

Some artistic special effects are better than others. Even the best are not the same as if they had been created with the corresponding artistic materials.

Fun

The Fun effects concentrate on altering the elements within an image, rather than just the colours and textures. The Fun effects can be created in the same way as the artistic ones: select an option, then enter values into a dialog box to specify the degree to which that effect will be applied.

If you are using the Distort special effects on a portrait of an individual, make sure that you know their sense of humour — no-one likes to be confronted by what they may think of as an embarrassing image of themselves.

Distort

This lets you distort an image to give it a weird and wonderful appearance. There are several options:

Pinch

Sphere

The Pond Ripple effect can be particularly striking if you select the water element of an image and apply the effect only to this.

Twirl

Pond Ripple

Diffuse

Motion

This can be used to create the effect of motion. It can be particularly useful for people involved in a sport or for vehicles:

The effect of motion can also be created by selecting an object in an image, then selecting Effects>Blur>Motion Blur from the Advanced Menu bar. Values can then be entered into the dialog box and the direction of the motion blur can be selected.

Perspective

This can be used to change the scale of items:

When applying special effects to images, make sure that the effect is relevant to the objects in an image i.e. motion effect for a car and a perspective effect for a building.

Negative

This creates the impression of a photographic negative:

Cloud Texture

This creates the effect of a hazy, cloudlike texture over an image. You can select specific colours for the effect:

Depending on the Background and Foreground colours you select for the Cloud texture, this can look more like a neon effect than a cloud one.

Chrome

This gives the objects in an image a chrome appearance:

The Chrome effect is best used on objects. If it is used on people it can result in some very strange effects. Useful perhaps if you want to create a science-fiction look.

Neon Glow

This makes an image appear as if it is under a neon light:

Patchwork

This creates the effect of an image having been constructed from dozens of little squares of colour:

Funnel

This converts an image into a funnel shape:

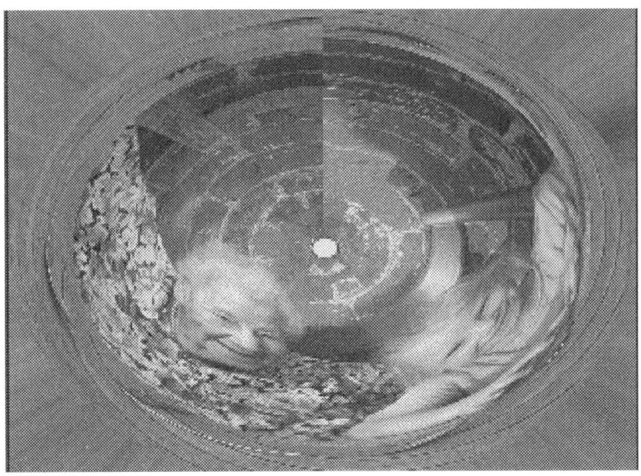

You will probably have to think quite creatively to think of a good use for the Funnel special effect. If you want to use this, keep its attributes in mind when you are capturing your images.

Textures

These effects can be used to give images the appearance of being created with artistic materials rather than just being two dimensional objects.

Choose a dark grey or dark red colour for the bas-relief effect if you want it to look like plaster or stone. Choose a brighter colour if you want to create a more surreal effect.

Bas Relief

This creates an effect as if the image has been created with plaster or stone:

If you are using the Note Paper effect, try printing the final result on actual notepaper. This will add to the overall effect.

Note Paper

This gives an image the appearance of being created on textured writing paper:

Crackle

This creates an effect of an old oil painting on canvas:

Solarize

This dramatically alters the colours in an image, to give it a surreal glow:

Sponge

BEWARE

The Sponge effect is not always the most effective and it can just make an image look blotchy.

This makes the image look as if it has been created with sponge painting:

Emboss

This gives an image a raised effect, as if it is a three-dimensional object:

Accent Elements

The Accent Elements can be applied to elements within images rather than the whole image. For these effects, the relevant object has to be selected before the effect is applied.

Drop Shadow

Drop shadows are a popular way to emphasise text, but to do this you would have to create a block of text as a graphical object rather than just a text block.

This applies an emphatic/artistic shadow effect:

Feather

This can be used to soften the edges around a selected object by blurring then slightly:

Feathering can be used to merge items to which motion blur has been added. Experiment with the level of feathering, to try and blend the selected object in with the rest of the image.

Silhouette

This creates a silhouette of the selected image which can be left blank or filled with a colour or a pattern:

Lighting Effects

This is an excellent option for highlighting elements of an image through the use of special lighting effects:

1. Select Lighting Effects in the Accent Element menu and select the Lighting Effects tab and then the Lighting Effects button

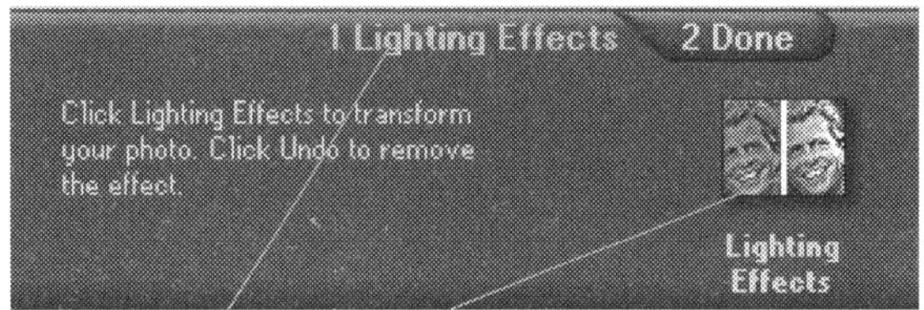

The options for the style of lighting effect that can be applied are:

- *Spotlight*
- *Coloured Spotlights*
- *Crossing Down*
- *Crossing Up*
- *Flashlight*
- *Floodlight*
- *Overall*
- *Three Lights Down*
- *Three Lights Up*

2. Select the style of lighting effect, its direction, its colour, its brightness and its size. Click OK to apply the effect

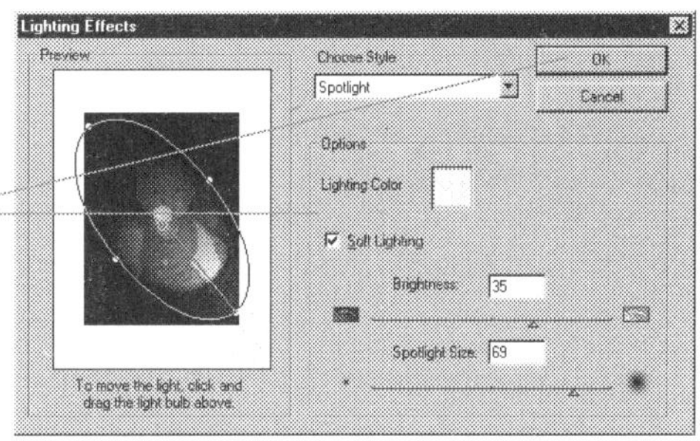

3. The selected lighting effect is applied to the image

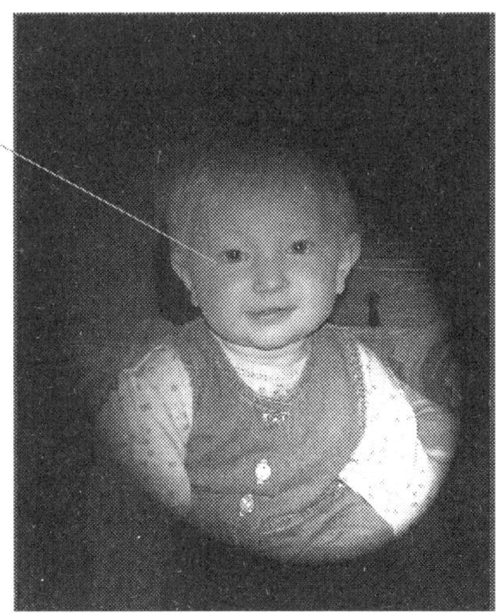

Make Transparent

This can be used to make some, or all, of an image transparent:

For some special effects, PhotoDeluxe automatically makes a copy of your image to work on, so that if you make any mistake you will always have the original. If a copy has been made, a text box will appear from the right hand margin alerting you to this.

Accented Edges

This can be used to emphasis the edges of items within an image:

The Color Eye effect can also be used to remove red-eye as well as the feature specifically designed for this purpose. If you are using this, make sure that you zoom in on the eye as much as possible as it will enable you to recolour individual pixels of colour, if required.

Color Eye

This can be used to change the colour of someone's eyes, by zooming in, selecting the pupil and then applying a new colour:

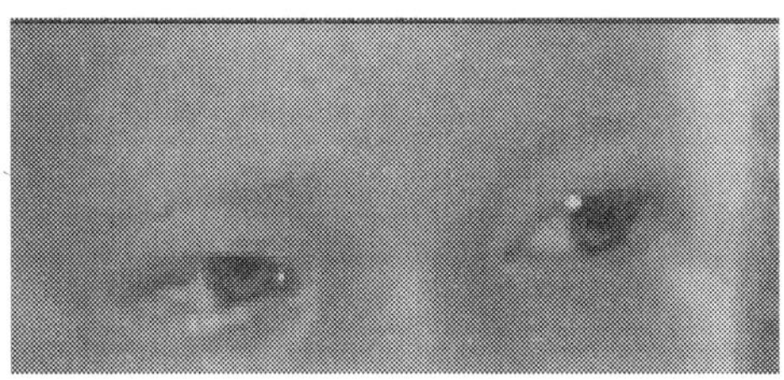

Re-Color Photo

This has three effects for altering the colours within images.

Coloring Book

This allows you to create outlines within an image and then colour in different segments, as you would with a child's colouring book:

1. Select Re-color Photo>Coloring Book

The Coloring Book effect is a good way to let children learn about digital images and at the same time let them indulge their liking for colouring in.

2. Click here to convert the image into a black and white sketch

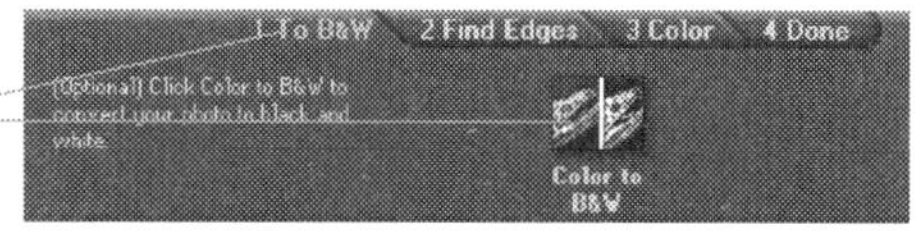

3. Click here to select the edges within the image. This will create areas that can then be coloured

Use an image that has a good colour contrast between the various elements. This will make it more effective when the edges are selected to create the outlines to be coloured.

4. Select the Paint tool to colour areas of the image and the Eraser to remove any mistakes. Click Done to save your changes

Hand Color

This is similar to the Coloring Book effect, except that the edges of the image are not selected to create outlines within it:

Images can be quickly converted into black and white by selecting Effects>Color to Black/White from the Advanced Menu bar.

Sketch

This creates a sketch effect by converting an image into black and white and then finding the edges. However, unlike the Coloring Book effect, it does not then allow for colouring it and leaves the outlines as they are:

Edge Effects

This contains two effects that are applied around the image rather than changing any of the elements within the image itself. It is similar to applying effects to a hard copy image.

The amount of page curl that is applies cannot be altered, so if you do not like the end result there is no way of changing it.

Page Curl

This creates the effect of turning up one corner of the image:

The Vignette effect is very useful for portrait images that are going to be printed and then placed in a frame. The Oval or the Rectangle selection tool can be used to select an area that corresponds to the size and shape of frame that is going to be used.

Vignette

This can be used to select a part of an image, remove the background and then soften the edges around the selected area:

Collage

The Collage effects can be used to combine elements from different images to create trick effects such as people appearing to be the same size as buildings. The basics of creating a collage are similar for each effect: select an initial image, select a background, combine the images and resize as required.

When dealing with collages, make sure that both of the images used have similar lighting conditions in terms of brightness and contrast. If necessary, edit the images before you begin using them for the collage.

Trick Scale

This can be used to create collages where objects appear unnaturally large or small:

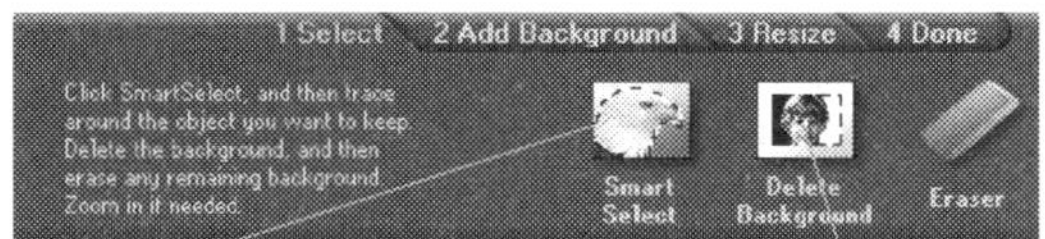

1. Select Special Effects>Collage>Trick Scale. Click on the SmartSelect button to select an object. Once it has been selected, click on Delete Background to remove the area behind the selected image

When creating Trick Scale collages, capture the original images with this in mind. If you want to use people in a particular image, such as leaning or kneeling, make sure that they pose in this way when you take the picture.

2. Select Add Background and then select an image that you want to serve as the background

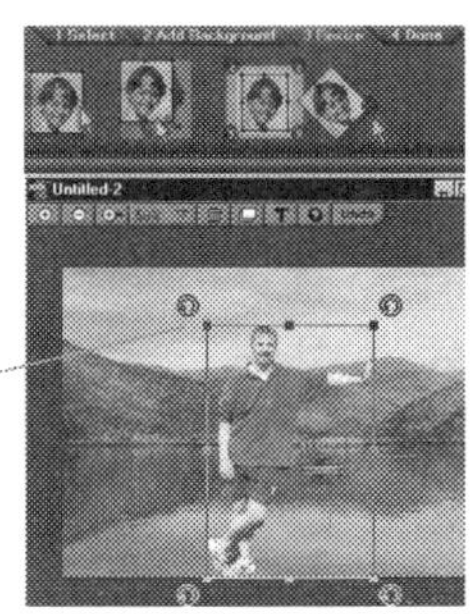

3. Click the Resize tab and resize the selected item on the background. Select Done when the desired effect has been achieved

Disguise Your Face

This adds clip art images to faces and people:

To create a disguise collage, select the image that you want to add the clip art to. Select the Clip Art icon and choose an item from the Photo Disguise library that you want to include. You will have to insert the PhotoDeluxe CD in order to access the clip art gallery.

Change Background

This allows you to combine two images so that one appears on an incongruous background:

The procedure for Change Background is similar to that for creating a Trick Scale collage.

Body Switch

This can be used to put a different head on a body:

Background Effects

This can be used to place the subject of an image on a patterned background:

Composite collages are created by opening a blank file and then adding as many images as required. These can then be resized accordingly. The Layers tab can then be used to arrange images above or below one another.

Composites

This can be used to combine several images in a collage rather than just two:

Creative projects

One of the main features of PhotoDeluxe is its ability to create a variety of projects such as cards and gift tags. This chapter shows some of the projects that can be undertaken and how to achieve some creative effects.

Covers

Chapter Nine

Cards

All of the creative projects are accessed from the Cards & More toolbar.

Probably the most commonly used project in PhotoDeluxe is the one for creating cards. There are several styles and designs that can be used:

If a step is not completed properly, a dialog box will appear telling you that you cannot move on to the next step.

1. Select Cards and the type of card you want to create

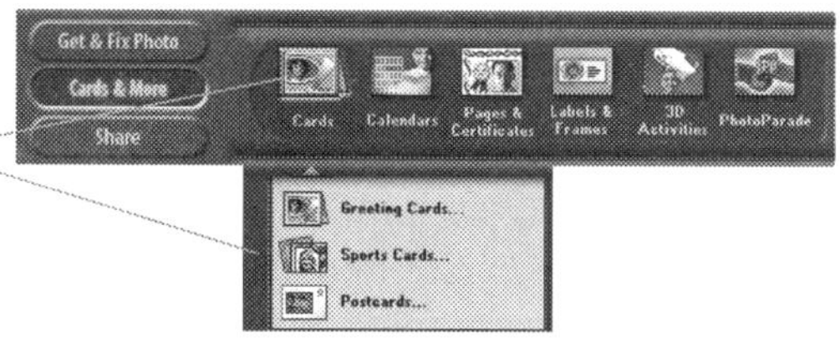

2. Select the Layout tab and choose a layout style

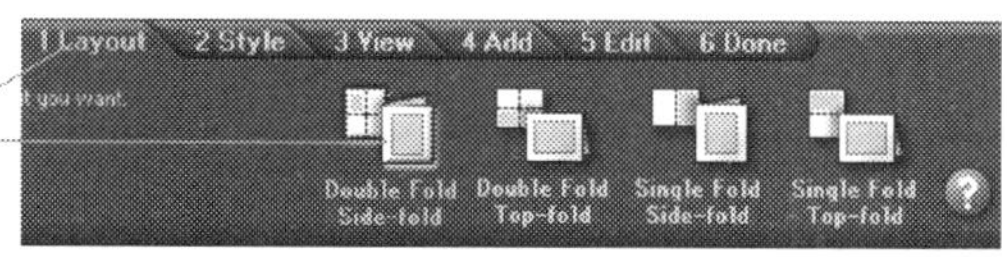

The PhotoDeluxe CD-ROM has to be inserted in order to load the image templates for the creation of cards.

3. Select the Style tab and then the Choose Style button. Double-click a template for the type of card you want to create

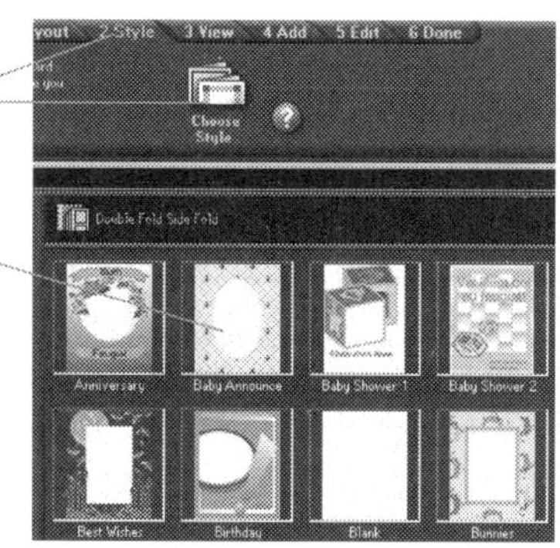

4 Select View and select Front, Back or Inside to view the different parts of the card

Some of the steps during the creation of cards can be processor intensive and take a few seconds to complete.

5 Select the Add tab and select an image from the usual sources

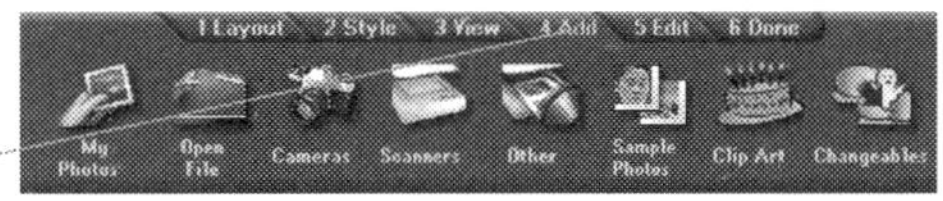

6 Once the image has been inserted into the card layout it can then be edited by selecting the Edit tab and the Done tab and then using the options from the Get & Fix Photo toolbar

When printing cards, use as good quality paper as possible. This will ensure that they have a more professional and sturdy appearance.

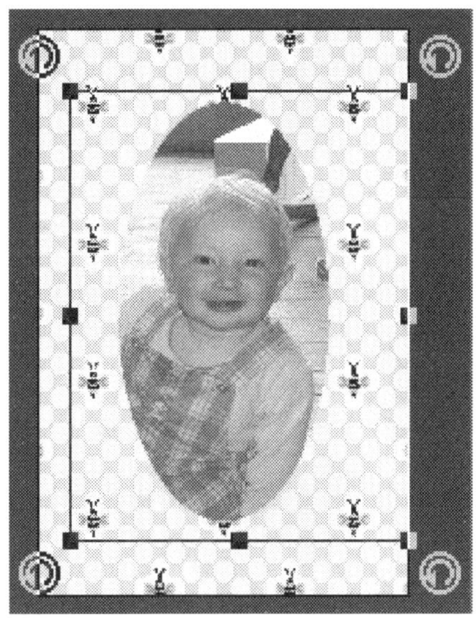

Calendars

Calendars can be created on a monthly or yearly scale:

Artistically created calendars that are mounted or framed make excellent presents. If you are doing this though, make sure that they are printed at as high a quality as possible. For more information on printing images, see Chapter Ten.

1. Select Calendars and the type of calendar you want to create

Even if you only want to create a monthly calendar, you will still have to select a year so that the correct days and dates can be created for that month.

2. Select the Month tab, the Month button and the month you want to use for the calendar. Select OK

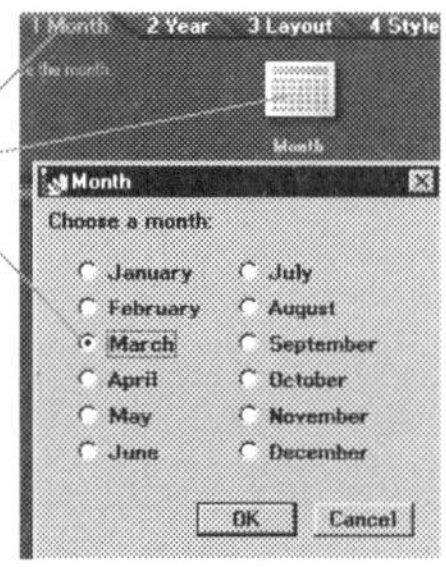

3. Select the Year tab and a year for your calendar

When a new layout is selected, it automatically opens up a new file with that layout as the background.

4. Select the Layout tab and the Choose Layout button. Double-click on a layout to open it, or drag it onto the work area

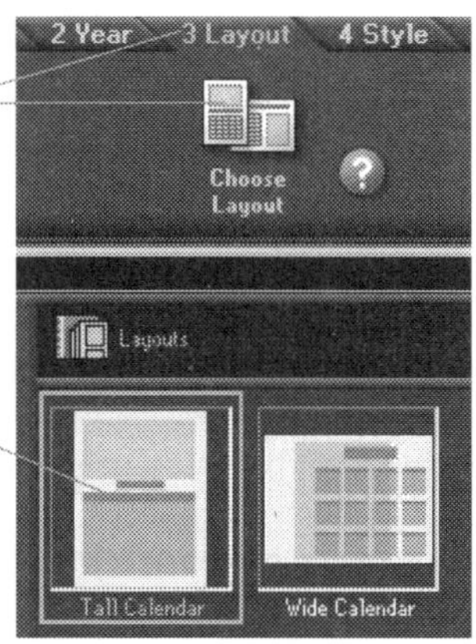

To use the layout and style options, the PhotoDeluxe CD-ROM has to be inserted as this is where the images are taken from.

5 Select the Style tab and the Choose Style button and select a style for your calendar by double-clicking on it or dragging it onto your open file

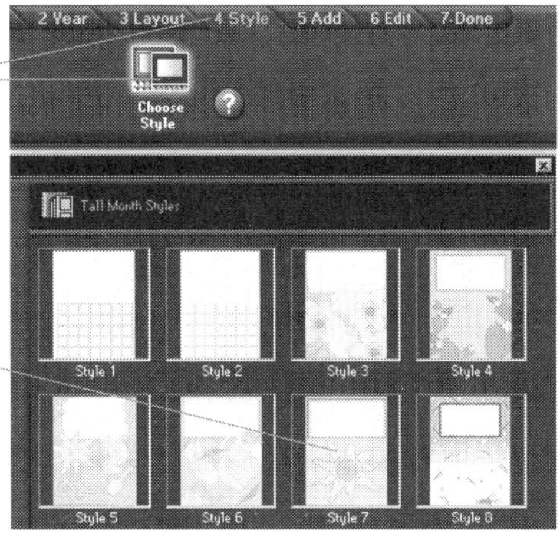

If you are creating a calendar for a particular month, then the Changeables or Clip Art can be useful options when you are adding images.

6 Select the Add tab and select an image from one of the usual sources

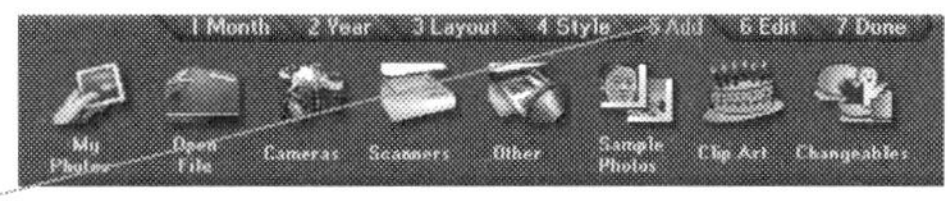

7 To edit the image in your card, select the Edit tab and the Done tab and then use the options from the Get & Fix Photo toolbar

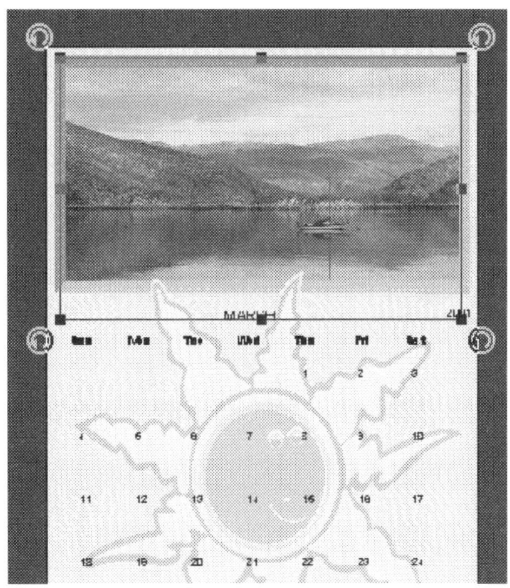

Pages & Certificates

The Pages & Certificates option covers various miscellaneous projects that are not really catered for under other headings. These include: Photo Albums, Signs, Covers, Certificates and Stationery. The procedure for creating each item is similar: choose the type of design you want, add an image and then edit it if required. The following example is for a photo album:

1. Select Pages & Certificates>Photo Albums from the Cards & More toolbar

When adding images to the photo album templates, they are placed on a layer behind the templates, so that the whole design of the template is visible.

2. Select the Choose Photo Album tab and Choose Page. Then double-click a design for your photo album

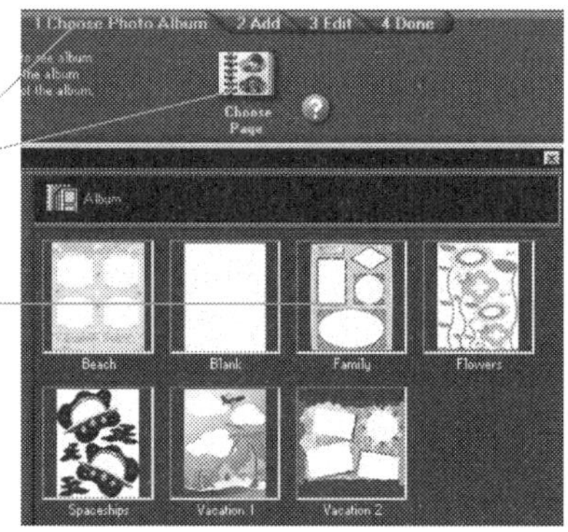

As with all projects, images can be added to Pages & Certificates by dragging them from the Open Photo panel, above the Advanced Menu button.

3. Select the Add tab to include images from the usual sources

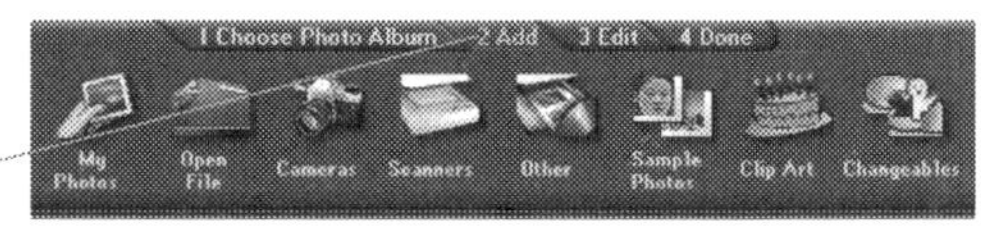

4. To edit the image in your card, select the Edit tab and the Done tab. Use the options from the Get & Fix Photo toolbar

Labels & Frames

This contains projects for creating items such as labels, photo frames, gift tags and magnets. The procedure for each is similar to that for Pages & Certificates. The following example is for creating labels:

Another option under Frames and Labels is for putting your images onto T-shirts. The procedure is the same for the other items in this category, except for when you print out your completed image. It has to be printed onto special T-shirt transfer paper which then can be applied to clothing by using an iron. T-shirt transfer paper can be bought at any computer accessories outlet that stocks a good range of computer paper.

Select File>Print Multiple from the Menu bar to print several copies of a label on a single sheet of paper. You can specify the number of copies that you want on a page in the print dialog box.

1. Select Labels & Frames>Labels from the Cards & More toolbar

2. Select the Choose Label tab and the Choose Label button. Then double-click a design for your label

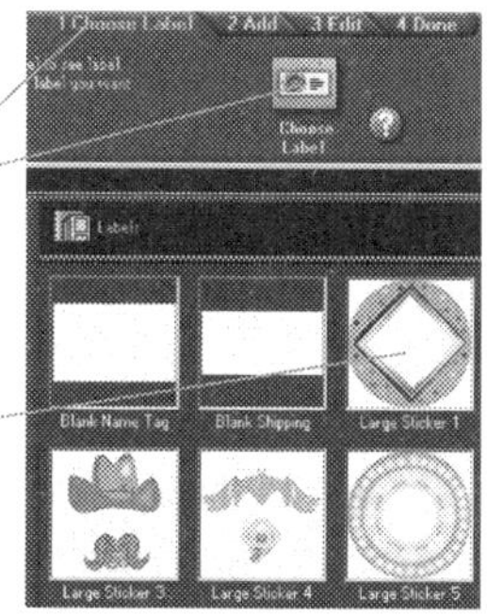

3. Select the Add tab to include images from the usual sources

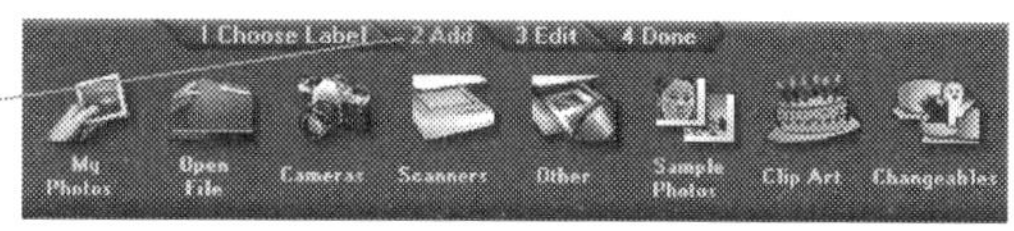

4. To edit the image in your label, select the Edit tab and the Done tab and then use the options from the Get & Fix Photo toolbar

3-D Activities

This is a new feature to PhotoDeluxe 4.0 for Windows and it allows you to combine your own images with 3-D clip art images. This is a valuable feature because it allows you to create more original effects than with two dimensional clip art. There is an extensive gallery of 3-D clip art images and it is a good idea to have a look at these if you are feeling creative. To create a 3-D project:

When you first start using 3-D Activities it is easy to get carried away and use this in every way imaginable. However, try and restrain yourself from using it too much as everyone else may not share you passion for this type of imagery. Use it sparingly and for effect.

1. Select 3-D Activities>Create 3-D Clip Art from the Cards & More toolbar

2. Select the Instructions tab for information about the procedure you are about to undertake

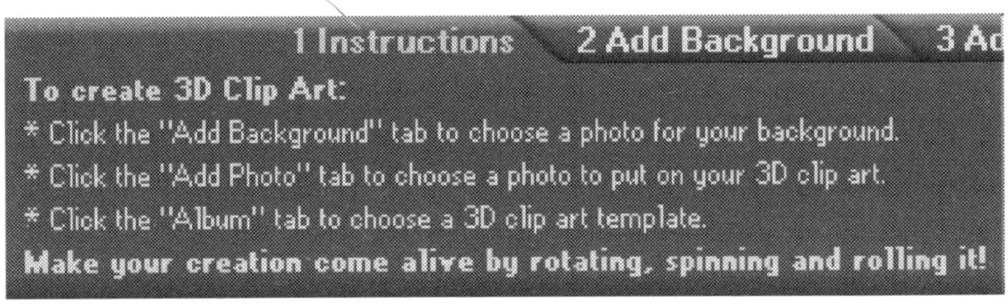

You do not have to have a background to create a 3-D project. Both steps are optional, but you have to select at least one of them. In some cases it is more effective to have a background image and a main photograph.

3. Select the Add Background tab to include images from the usual sources

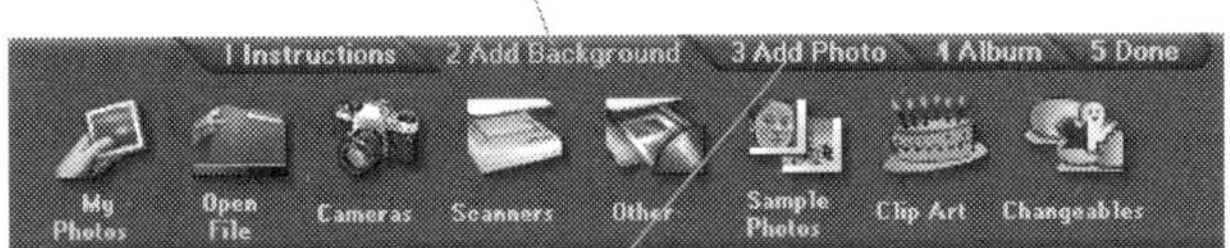

4. Select the Add Photo tab to include images from the usual sources

The 3-D object always sits on top of any background image that has been selected — it is the Add Photo image that is incorporated into the 3-D design.

5 Select the Album tab and Open Album to access the 3-D clip art collection. Double-click on an image to open it

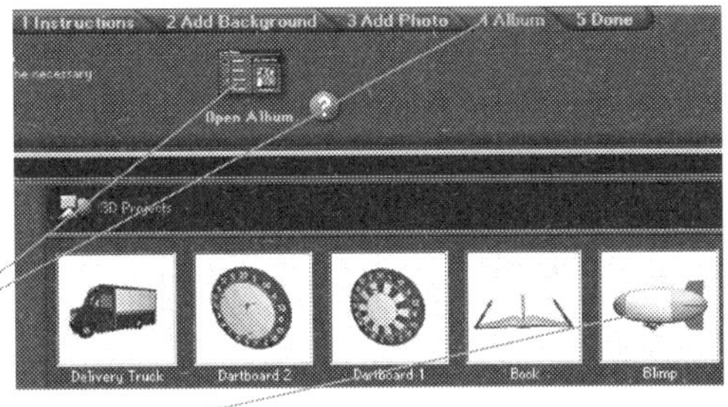

To find out more information about Kazoo and their 3-D technology, visit their Website at:

- *http://www.kazoo3d.com*

6 Once an item of 3-D clip art has been selected, it becomes incorporated into the images that have been selected. The result appears in the Kazoo 3-D Player, which is the format PhotoDeluxe uses to create 3-D images

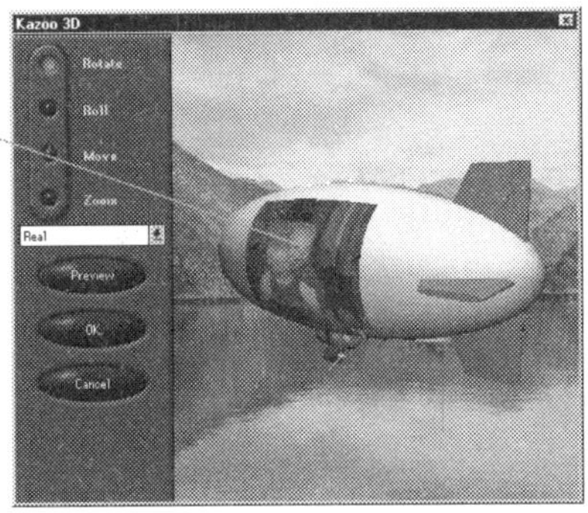

To Rotate, Roll or Move the 3-D object, click and drag on the image with the mouse. The image will move in the direction that you drag.

7 Select the Rotate, Roll or Move buttons to alter the appearance of the image

8 Select OK to save the 3-D image

3-D images are saved in the Kazoo format, which has a '.kzp' file extension. To view Kazoo 3-D objects, select Cards & More>3-D Activities>View 3-D Clip Art.*

PhotoParade

PhotoParade is an activity that creates on-screen slide shows with your images. In addition to linking them together it also has the facility to add themes and special effects. To create a PhotoParade:

PhotoParade slide shows can be used for family occasions or for a distraction during events such as children's birthday parties.

1. Select PhotoParade>Create a PhotoParade from the Cards & More toolbar

2. Select the Album tab and the Open Album button and make sure that the PhotoParade button is selected in the My Photos window

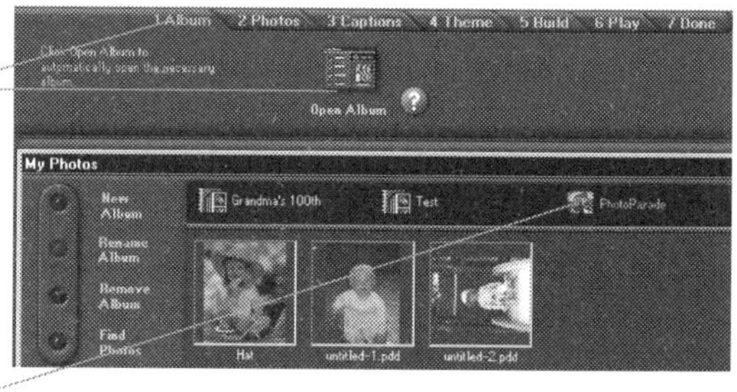

PhotoParade presentations can consist of images in several different formats. As long as an image can be opened in PhotoDeluxe, then it can be added to a PhotoParade.

3. Select the Photos tab and the Add Photo button

You can create PhotoParade slide shows with dozens of images, but remember that your audience may not share your own views about watching your holiday snaps on-screen.

4. Add all of the images that you want to be displayed in the PhotoParade

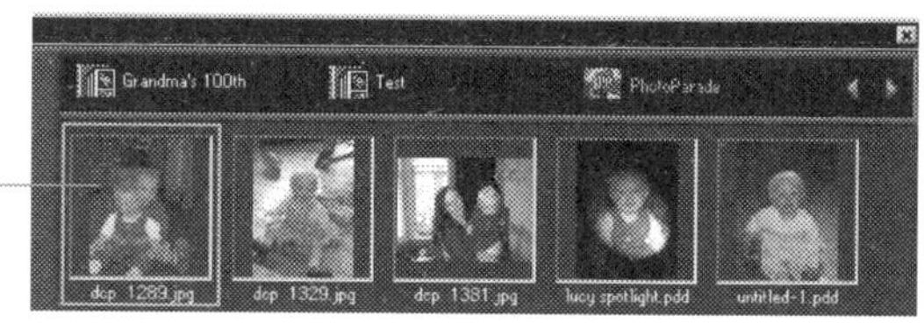

5 Select the Captions tab and the Add Caption button

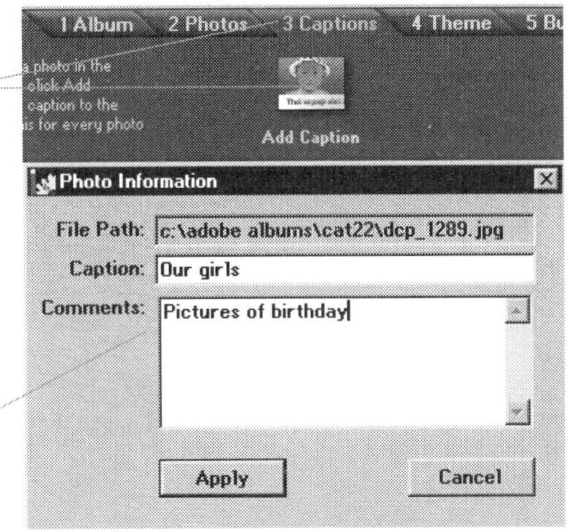

6 Enter a name and, if required, a comment for each image in your PhotoParade

When adding captions and comments, each image has to be selected in turn and then the Add Caption button selected.

7 Select the Theme tab and click here to access the available themes. Select one and view a thumbnail preview here

If you are going to be displaying your presentation on your own PC, leave the Segment Size option at Unsegmented, which keeps all of the images together. If you are going to email it to someone, select 1 Mb, as some Internet Service Providers do not allow files larger than this to be sent.

If you are going to save it to a floppy disc, select 1.4 Mb Floppy. The end user can then save all of the files onto their own hard drive. When they play the PhotoParade it will automatically play from the beginning.

8 Select the Build tab and the Build PhotoParade button to create your presentation

9 Save your PhotoParade. This will be done with the PhotoParade file extension, which is '*.php'

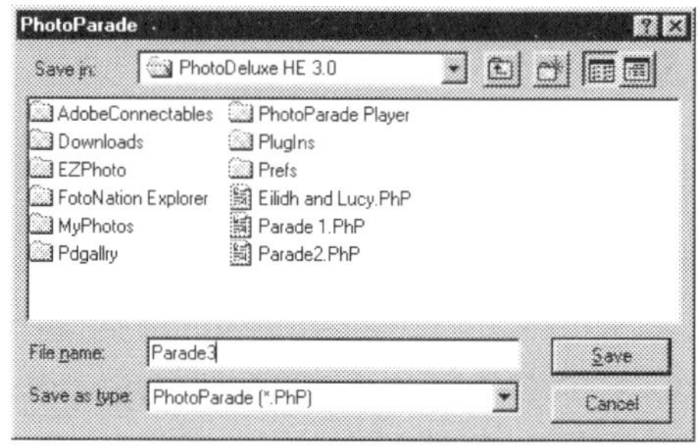

To find out more information about PhotoParade visit their Website at:

- *http://www.photoparade .com*

10 Select the Play tab and the Play a PhotoParade button to view the finished slide show. Select Done to finish the PhotoParade activity

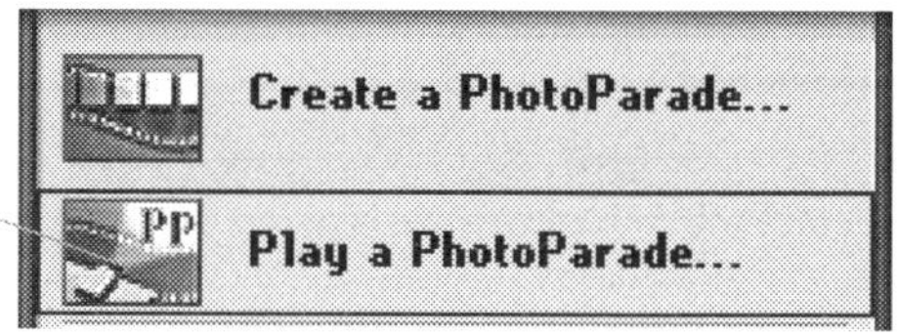

Press the Esc key at any time to stop a PhotoParade presentation playing.

Playing a PhotoParade presentation

PhotoParade presentations can be played at any time, as follows:

1 Select PhotoParade>Play a PhotoParade from the Cards & More toolbar

If you want to view your presentation without the attached theme, select Esc and select Carousel>Play.

2 Select a PhotoParade presentation from your hard drive. Click on Open to play the PhotoParade

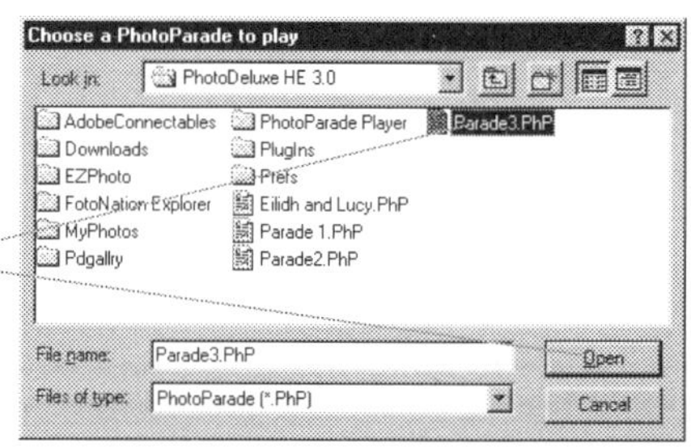

Printing images

This chapter looks at how images can be printed from PhotoDeluxe. It deals with some general issues about printing digital images and shows how to create the best looking images from PhotoDeluxe, using printer settings and colour matching techniques.

Covers

Chapter Ten

Choosing a printer

If you are going to be producing hard copies of your digital images then a good quality printer is essential: there is little point in carefully capturing and editing your images only to be let down by the printing process. When choosing a printer for colour images there are two main choices:

For more information about some of the leading printer manufacturers, look at the following Websites:

- *Canon – http://www.canon.com*
- *Epson – http://www.epson.com*
- *Hewlett Packard – http://www.hp.com*

- Inkjet
- Laser

While colour laser printers produce the best results, they are prohibitively expensive for the average home user. Therefore inkjet printers are the best option.

Inkjet is a name that was first used by Hewlett Packard to describe a particular process of getting ink from a printer onto the paper. Since then, other major printer manufacturers, such as Canon and Epson have created similar technologies (bubblejet for Canon and micro piezon for Epson). However, the term inkjet is still generally used for this type of printer. All of the inkjet methods work in a similar way: tiny dots of coloured ink are placed onto the paper by a collection of miniature nozzles. This is usually done with two cartridges, one containing black ink and the other containing cyan, magenta and yellow. When they are combined they create the CMYK (K is for black) colour model.

Some colour inkjet printers have an additional two colours in the colour cartridge (lighter shades of magenta and cyan). This increases the colour variations available and is particularly effective for subtle colour changes such as skin tones.

The price of inkjet printers has fallen dramatically in recent years and it is possible to get an excellent one for under £200. This should have a very high print resolution (see next page) and be able to produce images that are nearly as good as hard copy photographs. At present it is not possible to match the quality of hard copy because you can always see the individual coloured dots that make up the image if you look closely enough. However, in the future the quality will undoubtedly get even better.

Printer resolution and speed

Resolution

The crucial factor governing the quality of the output from an inkjet printer is its resolution. This is measured in dots per inch (dpi) and it determines how many dots of colour are placed in each inch. The general standard is 300 dpi, but some of the higher quality printers go up to 1440 dpi. This does not affect the resolution of the image which remains the same regardless of the printer resolution. If you buy a printer that has a headline figure of 1440 dpi, you will also be able to set it to a lesser setting for draft printing. The best quality setting should only be used for the final version of an image.

The higher the printer resolution then the more ink will be used up. This should be kept in mind when considering the cost of the printer and the ink cartridges.

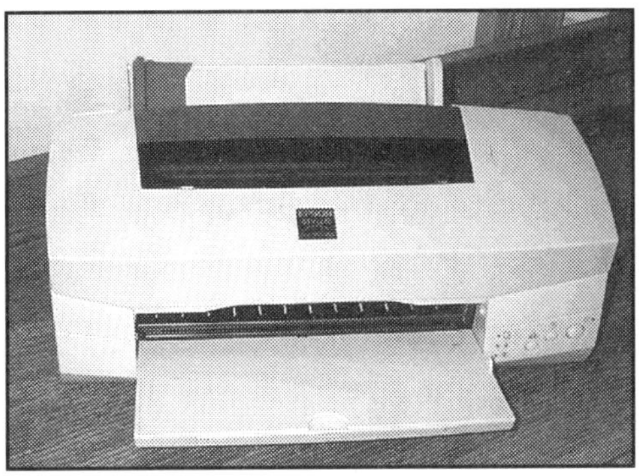

Top quality inkjet printers, such as the Epson Photo 750, can produce stunning photo-realistic results

When you are looking at printers, ask to see them in action. Make sure this is at their best setting and on photographic quality paper. Most printers have display images with them, but this is not the same as seeing them print something in front of you.

Speed

Another selling point for inkjet printers is the speed at which they print pages (pages per minute). If you are going to be printing a lot of long text-based documents then this could be an issue. However, the printing of digital images is usually a more leisurely pursuit and quality is of greater concern than speed. In some cases it may even be beneficial if printers took a bit longer, to increase the output quality. In any case, the pages per minute figure can be misleading as this is usually for black and white printing at draft quality. If you are concerned about the output speed, ask how many pages per minute the printer can produce in colour at top quality.

Paper

When it comes to printing digital images the issue of paper types is a vital one. Inkjet printers can achieve reasonable results on plain, multi-purpose A4 paper, but if you use more specialised paper then the difference can be dramatic.

Photographic quality paper is designed to grip the ink more securely so that there is less chance of dots blurring into each other.

Some of the types of paper that can be used for printing digital images are:

- Standard multi-copy paper. This can be used in most types of printers as well as fax machines and photocopiers. It is versatile, but gives the poorest quality for digital images
- Inkjet paper. This is the next step up from multi-copy paper and gives excellent results with items with solid blocks of colour such as charts and logos

In addition to the photographic paper from the branded digital imaging companies, there are a lot of other companies producing this type of paper. Experiment with different ones to see which give the best results.

- Photographic quality paper. This is a generic term for thicker, glossy paper that produces the best results with digital images on a colour inkjet printer. It is the most expensive type of paper but it should definitely be used when you are printing the final version of an image
- Specialised paper. This includes postcard size photographic paper for images that you want to put in an album, or T-shirt transfers. These can have images printed onto them and this can then be put onto an item of clothing using an iron

When using a T-shirt transfer, always test it on an old piece of clothing. Wasting one transfer will be less expensive than an unfortunate accident with your favourite T-shirt.

There is a wide array of paper for producing digital images — much of it from the main digital imaging companies

Ink

There can be a considerable difference in price between ink cartridges for different printers. Take this into consideration when you are buying a printer and ask how many pages, on average, a cartridge will be able to print.

Cartridges

In combination with the paper, the ink is the next most important part of producing printed digital images. The ink itself is usually of a similar quality between manufacturers. However, some printers come with an additional colour photographic cartridge. This can be inserted when you want to print out the best quality of your image. These cartridges are expensive but they do improve the quality of images. Not all printer manufacturers use them, and those who do not would argue that their printers give a top quality anyway. When looking at printers, ask to see examples of those that use a colour photographic cartridge to see if the quality warrants the additional cost.

If an inkjet printer is not used for several weeks, the ink cartridge nozzles could become clogged with dried up ink.

Colour photographic cartridges can improve the quality of images, but they are expensive

Due to the tendency of printed inkjet images to fade over time, it is essential that you keep a copy of the original so that you can print out another hardcopy if required.

Fading

It is a fact of digital life that images printed on inkjet printers fade over a period of time. Sunlight can have a particularly adverse effect and a printed image left in direct contact with this can begin to fade after only a few months. If this is avoided then the image could easily last two or three years before it begins to fade.

One way to increase the life-span of your printed images is to use a water-fast spray. These are available from most art shops and give a certain amount of general protection. Some types also give specific protection against sunlight.

Setting the print size

When printing images one of the first things you will want to do is to set the size at which they will be produced. This can be done by entering details for the size of the output image.

When setting the size for a printed image, the trick is to allow it to be printed at a reasonable size while still retaining an image resolution of at least 100 ppi or above.

(Sometimes this cannot be achieved without resampling — see the tip below).

Setting the size

To set the output print size of an image:

1 Select Size>Photo Size from the Advanced Menu bar

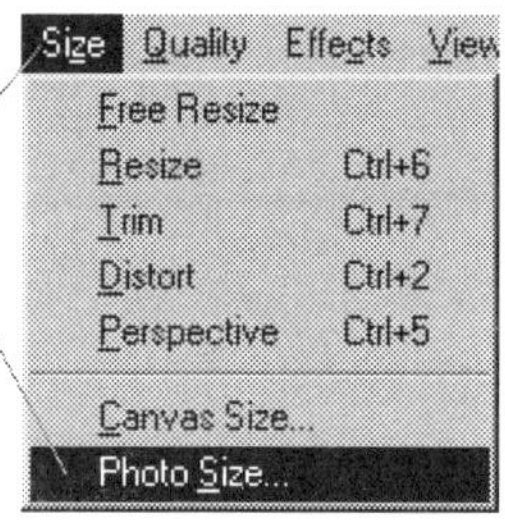

2 Enter new Width/Height values here for the required size of the output images

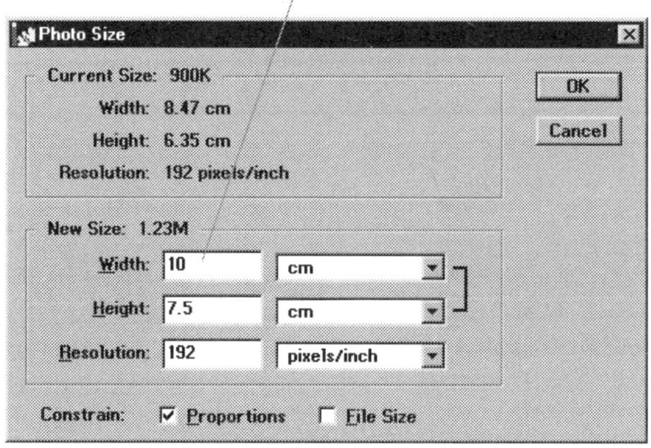

3 If the size of the image has been increased then each pixel has to cover a greater area than before. This can lead to an inferior quality in the final printed image

If you check off the Constrain> Proportions box in the Photo Size dialog box, then the print size of the image can be increased without decreasing the image resolution. This is known as resampling, which means PhotoDeluxe adds pixels to increase the size of the image while maintaining the same resolution. This is intended to keep the same quality when increasing the size of an image. However, this is not always the case as the pixels that are added are not as well defined as the ones that were captured in the original image. This can also create much larger file sizes.

Using preset sizes

It is possible to print an image within various standard paper sizes. To do this:

It is also possible to change the size of images by dragging them to make them larger or smaller. To do this, select Size>Free Resize from the Advanced Menu bar and then drag one of the resizing handles that appear.

1. Select Print>Print Standard Sizes from either the Get & Fix Photo or the Cards & More toolbars

The Paper Type that is chosen is not the size of the actual paper that the image will be printed on. It just acts as a frame into which the image can be placed. Once this has been done the image and the frame around it will appear superimposed on the paper size that has been selected for the printer setup (usually A4 by default).

2. Select the Style tab and choose to have a single image printed or include several

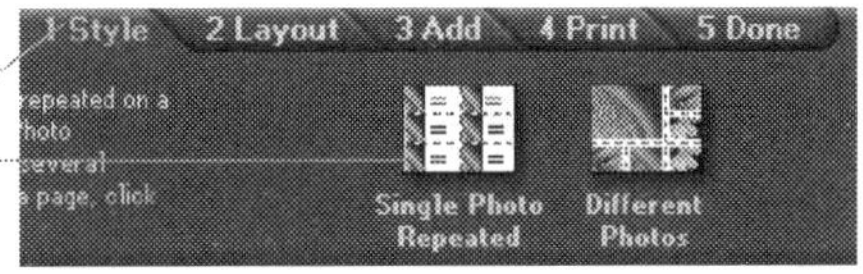

3. Select the Layout tab and Choose Layout button

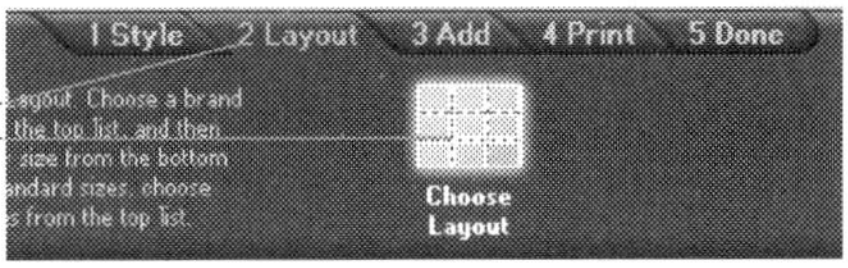

If you want to print a single image over a whole sheet of A4 paper, then resize it using the Size>Photo Size command from the Advanced Menu bar.

4. Select a paper type and size from the Choose Paper Type dialog box. Select OK

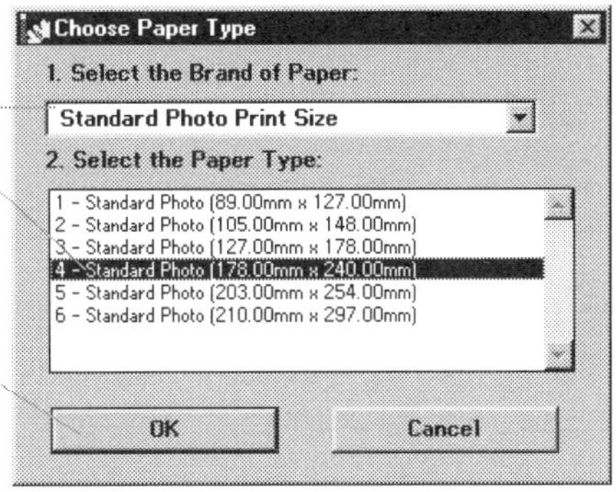

5 Select the Add tab and Preview button to see how the print image will look. To alter the number of copies that can be printed on the page, enter new values here

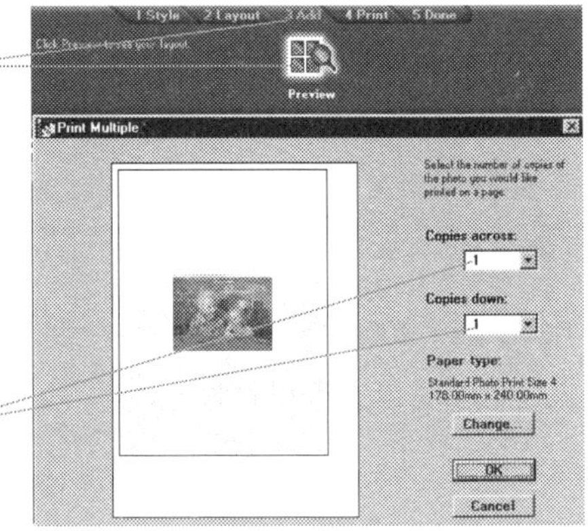

The print size of an image will be the same regardless of the size of paper that is selected for it.

6 Select the Print tab and the Print button to send the image to the printer

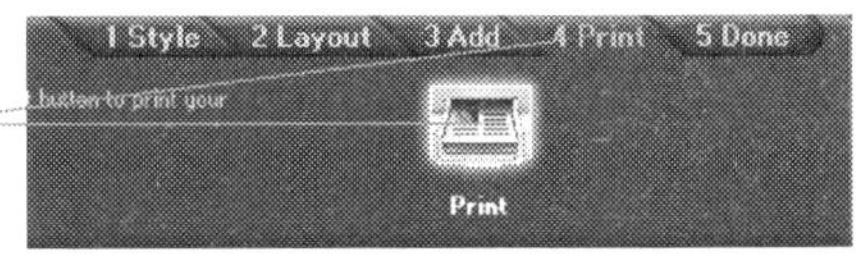

7 Select the required settings in the Print dialog box

For information about the settings in the Print dialog box, see page 159.

8 Select OK to print

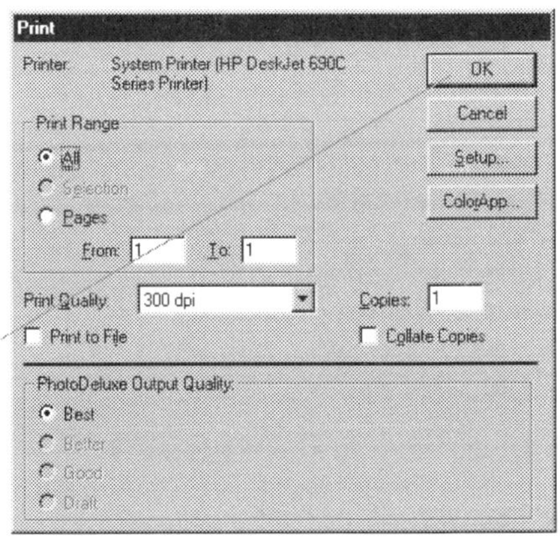

Previewing images and multiple copies

Previewing images

Before you print an image, it is important to preview the way it will look on the selected size of paper. This ensures that the image is not too big for the size of paper onto which it is going to be printed and it also gives an idea of the size of the image in relation to the output paper size. To preview how an image will appear when it is printed:

You can also preview an image by selecting File>Print Preview from the Menu bar.

1 Select Print>Print Preview from either the Get & Fix Photo or the Cards & More toolbars

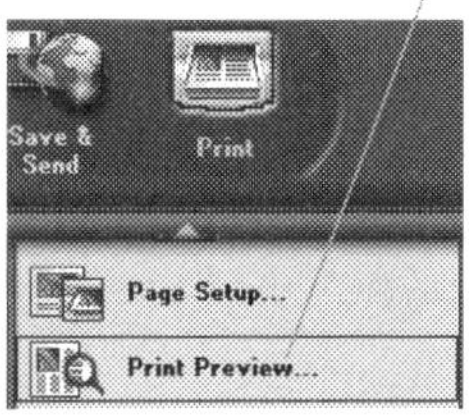

2 The image appears as it will on the selected paper size when it is printed

Printing multiple copies

It is possible to print several copies of the same image on a single sheet of paper. This can be an economical option if you have to print numerous copies. To do this:

When selecting the number of multiple copies to print on a single page, you will not be able to enter a number that would cause there to be too many images for the size of the paper.

1 Select Print>Print Multiple on a Page from either the Get & Fix Photo or the Cards & More toolbars

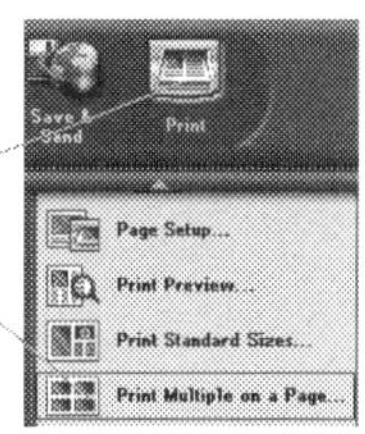

2 Enter values for the number of images you want printed across and down on the page

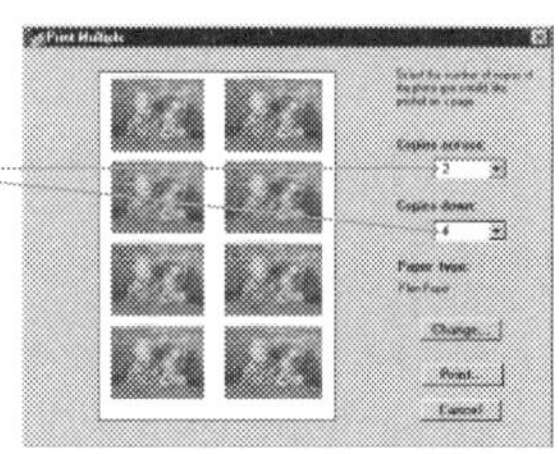

Page setup

Before you print an image it is necessary to set some details about the current page (or image) that will be sent to the printer by PhotoDeluxe when the print command is activated. This includes information such as:

- The type of printer
- The paper size
- The paper source
- The page orientation i.e. landscape or portrait

If the paper orientation is set to landscape, the page will print horizontally, and for portrait the page will print vertically.

Setting page setup information

1 Select Print>Page Setup from either the Get & Fix Photo or the Cards & More toolbars

The Page Setup dialog box can also be accessed by selecting File>Page Setup from the Menu bar.

2 In the Page Setup dialog box, enter the details for printer, paper size, paper source and orientation

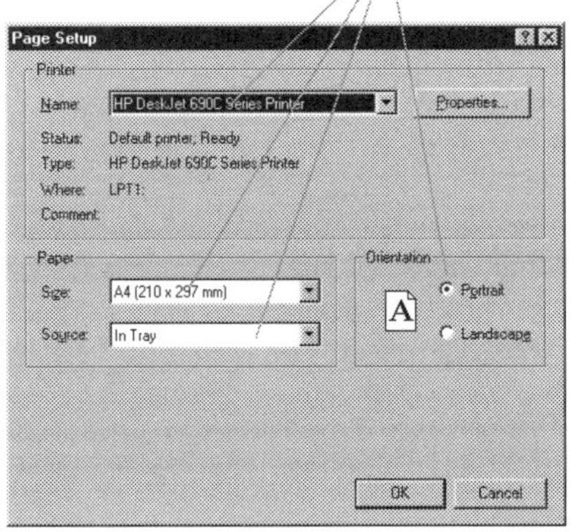

Printing

If it is done properly, printing an image is one of the most satisfying parts of working with digital images. The first step is to set the print properties. These tell the printer the type of paper that is being used and the output quality that is required (usually Draft, Good and Best, or similar). To set the print properties:

Although all printers are different, most of them have a similar method for setting the print properties as the one shown here. On some printers, these options may be available by selecting the Options button.

1 In the Page Setup dialog box, select the Properties button

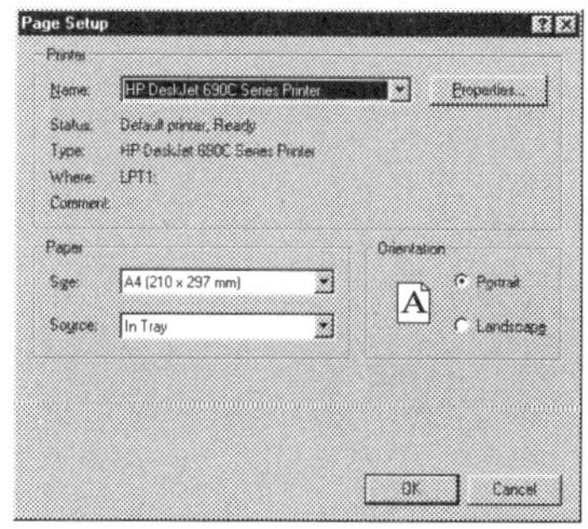

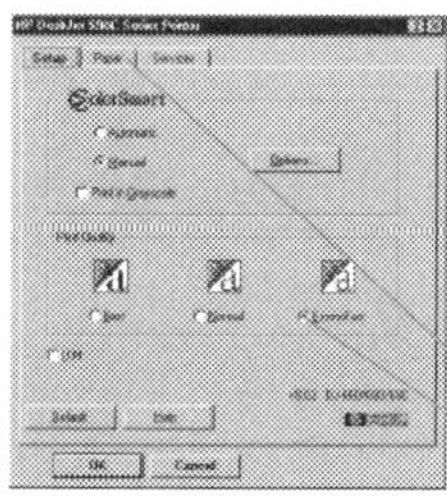

2 Select the print quality and the type of paper

Always print a draft version of your image on plain paper before you print a good quality one on photographic paper. This will ensure that you do not waste ink and paper if the printed version is not exactly as you had hoped.

Once the page setup and print properties have been set, the image can be printed:

1 Select Print>Print from either the Get & Fix Photo or the Cards & More toolbars

To print only a specific part of an image, select it with one of the selection tools. Then in the Page Range part of the Print dialog box, click on Selection. Select OK to print the selection.

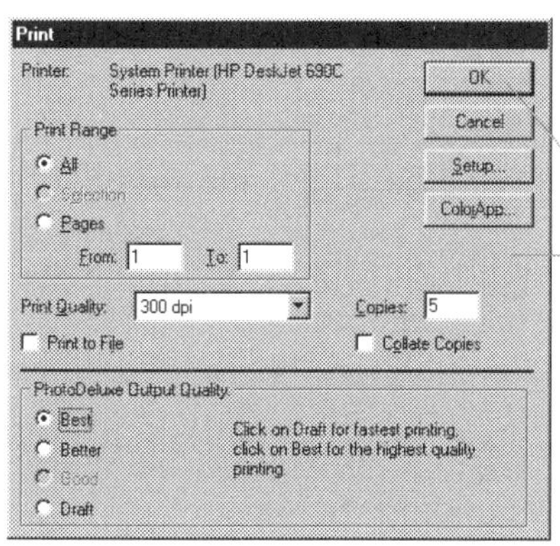

2 In the Print dialog box enter details for the page range, the number of copies, the output resolution and quality. Select OK to print

Matching colours

It is a fact of digital life that when an image is printed, the colours do not always match what appears on the computer monitor. To compensate for this, PhotoDeluxe has a function for matching on-screen colours with those that come out of the printer:

1 Select Print>Adjust Color Printing from either the Get & Fix Photo or the Cards & More toolbars

The Adjust Color Printing dialog box can also be accessed from the Print dialog box by selecting the ColorApp button.

2 In the Adjust Color Printing dialog box, check on Adjust color printing

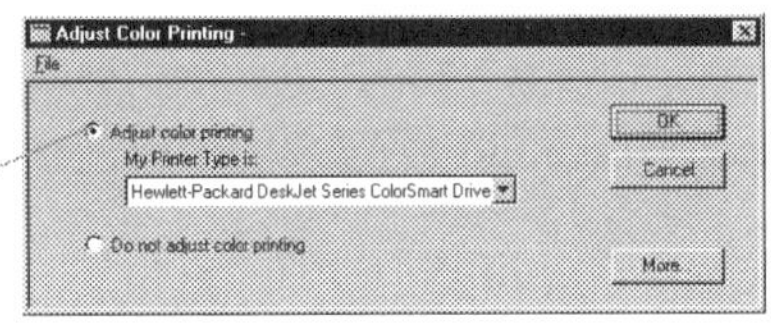

If your printer does not appear on the drop-down list, select Other.

3 Select the printer you are using from the drop-down list

4 Select More>Print to see thumbnail examples for the colour matching. Select the one that is the closest to the on-screen version. Select OK to have this applied to the full printed image

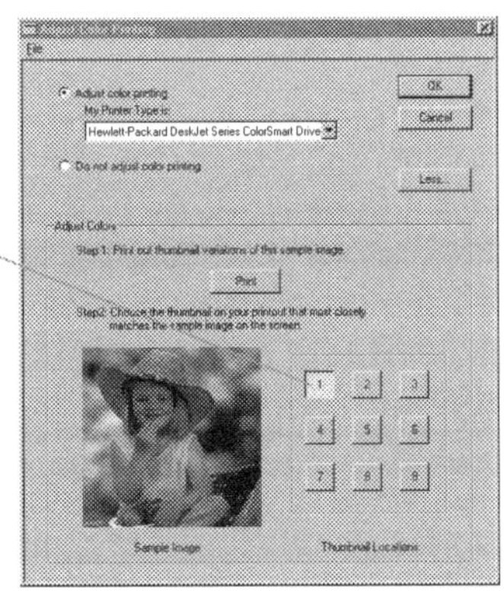

Sharing images

Sharing images is no longer confined to passing around well-thumbed snapshots. PhotoDeluxe specialises in enabling you to share your digital images via email or on the Web. This chapter looks at the sharing capabilities of PhotoDeluxe and how is works closely with another image sharing program, ActiveShare.

Covers

Chapter Eleven

Sharing with PhotoDeluxe

One of the main developments with PhotoDeluxe 4.0 is its image sharing capabilities. As more and more people become acquainted with the Internet, so the general awareness of sharing data becomes more widespread. This applies particularly to digital images since the Internet offers several options for letting people around the world see pictures that previously would have taken days to send by traditional mail. With PhotoDeluxe, images can be shared via email or through various options on the Web.

The various options for sharing images through PhotoDeluxe are:

- ActiveShare
- Email
- eCircles

Most of PhotoDeluxe's image sharing functions are centred around ActiveShare, which is an image editing program specifically designed for distributing images over the Web. This is the first option on the Share toolbar and for a more detailed look at ActiveShare, see page 168.

Accessing the sharing element of PhotoDeluxe

1 Select the Share toolbar and the Web Sharing button

2 Select a sharing activity from here

The Seasonal Sharing button on the Share toolbar is for seasonal activities that are triggered by the computer's clock. These activities can be downloaded from the PhotoDeluxe CD-ROM and updated from the Adobe Website at:

http://www.adobe.com

Email

Note that the other elements which form part of the Internet are:

- *the World Wide Web (WWW), the pages that individuals/organisations publish for the world to see*
- *newsgroups*
- *chat rooms*

When attaching a digital image to an email, make sure that the recipient has the means to read it. When emailing images, keep your files in a common format such as a JPEG or a GIF.

Always try and attach a file before you enter the email address, subject and header. Otherwise you may send the message without including the attachment.

Make sure your file sizes are as small as possible before emailing them. Otherwise they may take too long in downloading — some ISPs have a size limit for attachments.

Email was one of the first applications to revolutionise the Internet and it remains its most widely used element. However, it has advanced considerably since its early days, when to send a simple text message was considered a major breakthrough. Today email can be formatted in a variety of styles and be used to send attachments consisting of any type of computer file. Digital images are obviously ideal for this form of communication and it has enabled people to send image files around the world in a matter of a few seconds. To do this in PhotoDeluxe:

1. From the Share toolbar, select the Web Sharing button and then the Email button

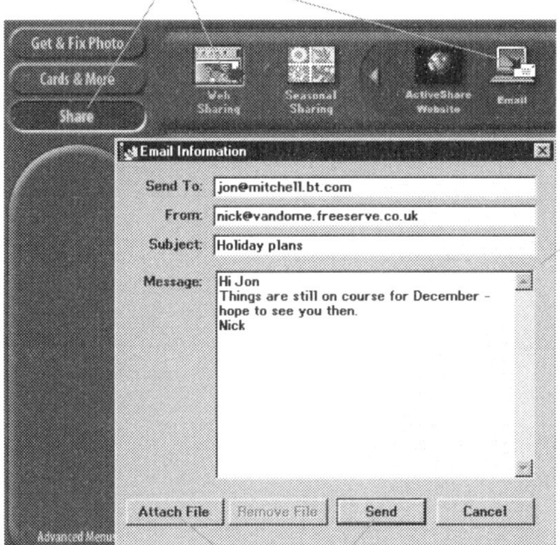

2. Enter the recipient's email address and your own and also the subject and any message

3. Select Attach File and select a file from your hard drive. Select Send to send the email message and the attachment to the recipient

Web projects

As well as offering facilities for simply sending images to other people or posting them on the Web, PhotoDeluxe also enables you to create digital postcards or puzzles and then post them on a private ActiveShare Website. You can then email other people and invite them to come and look at this site. To create a Web project:

Using the ActiveShare Website to post images and projects is completely free i.e. there is no registration fee.

1. From the Share toolbar, select the Web Sharing and Web Projects buttons

2. Select the Choose tab and either the Picture Postcard or the Picture Puzzle buttons

The Email dialog box for sharing a Web project does not have an option for attaching files, unlike the standard email function. This is because the current active image is used to create the project, whereas when you are emailing an image you have to select which one to send — it is not automatically the one on which you are currently working.

3. Select the Email tab and the Email Button. Enter the details of the people you want to invite to view your Web project. Select OK

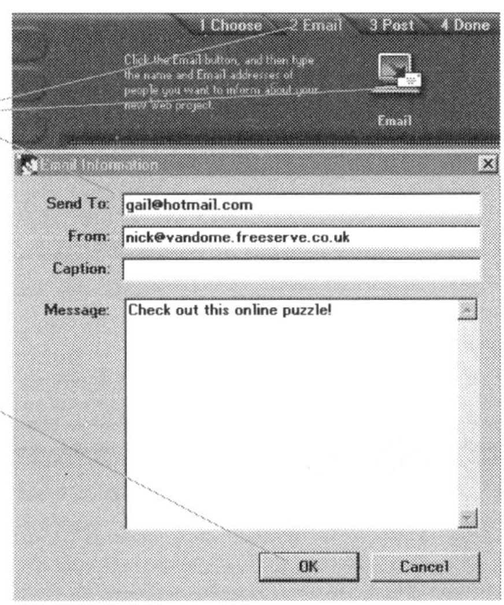

When you are creating a Web project, make sure your modem is connected and switched on, so that the project can be loaded onto the ActiveShare Website.

4 Select the Post tab and the Post to Web button

5 You will be connected to the ActiveShare Web login dialog box. Click here to login or click here if you have not already registered

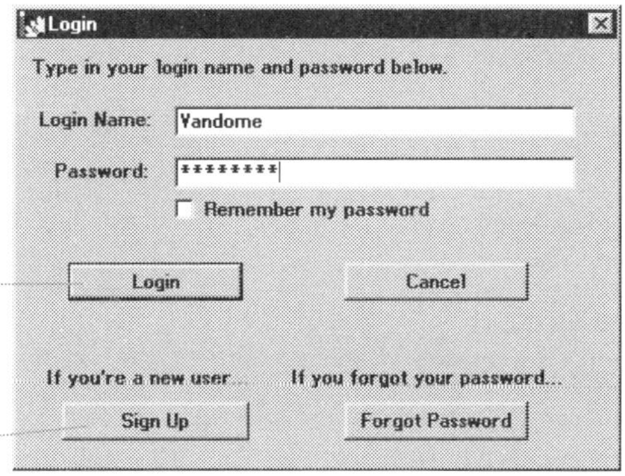

You can invite people to view your eCircle, and join it, by emailing directly from the eCircle itself. For more information on this, see page 183.

6 A window will appear telling you that the email recipients have been sent details of your project and where to find it on the Web. Select OK

Share on Web

The Share on Web function is similar to the Web Projects one, except that it just posts regular images rather than puzzles or postcards. To use Share on Web:

1 From the Share toolbar, select the Web Sharing button and then the Share on Web button

The Web Community option on the Web Sharing part of the Share toolbar takes you directly to the login page for ActiveShare's eCircles. Use this to access your current eCircles if you have already registered with ActiveShare or select the Sign Up button if you have not yet registered and created an eCircle.

2 Select the Open Web Album tab and then the Web Album button. This opens a window for organising the images that you are going to post to the Web

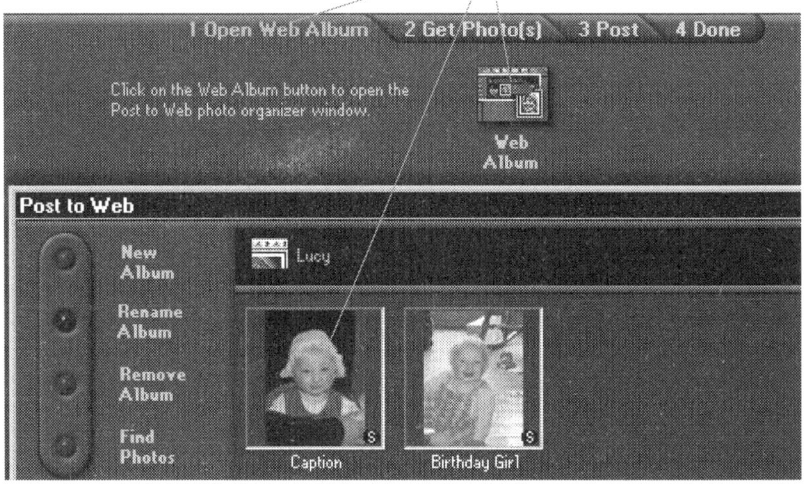

The Tell Me More option on the Web Sharing part of the Share toolbar connects to the ActiveShare Website and gives general information about eCircles and sharing images over the Web.

3 Select the Get Photo(s) tab and select My Photos. Open an album in My Photos and drag the images you want to use and drop them into the Post to Web organiser window

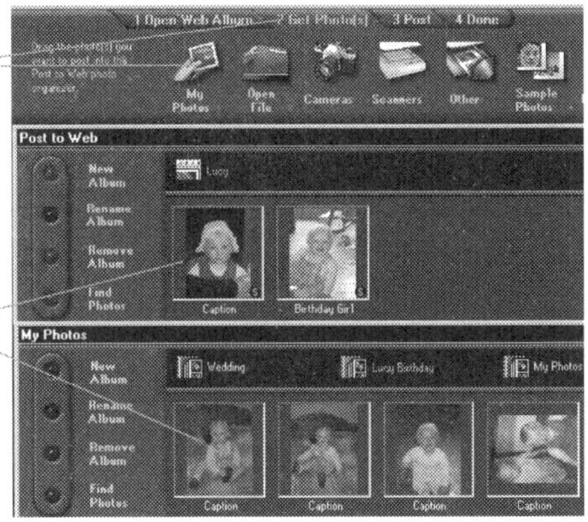

4 Select the Post tab and the Post to Web button

5 You will be connected to the ActiveShare Website. Click here to login, or click here if you have not already registered

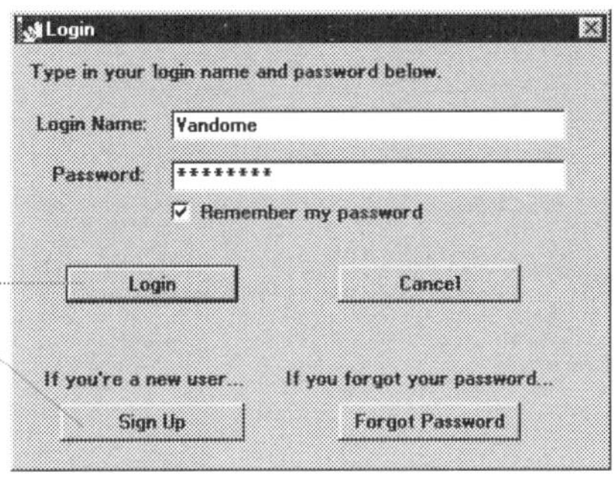

When opening images to include in the Post to Web organiser window, it is possible to open them from a source other than My Photos and drag and drop them from the main work area. However, this does not always work as effectively and so it is better to stick with the My Photos option if possible.

If you have already registered with ActiveShare and created some eCircles, you will be able to login at Step 5 and then specify to which of your eCircles you would like to post the images that you are uploading. Alternatively, you could create a new eCircle for them altogether. Once you have logged in, a dialog box appears with all of these options.

About ActiveShare

If you do want to create your own Web pages, Adobe have an excellent Web authoring package called PageMill. This creates Web pages without the need to know about HyperText Markup Language (HTML). For more information, see 'PageMill in easy steps'.

When PhotoDeluxe 4.0 was being developed Adobe discovered that the function users requested most was the ability to not only edit images, but also to share them on the Web. The solution to this is a program called Adobe ActiveShare. This allows users to post their images on the Web, without the need to create their own Websites. The images are placed within a password protected location and the user can then let their friends and family know the password, thereby creating a personalised image sharing site on the Web. PhotoDeluxe and ActiveShare work seamlessly together to allow users greater flexibility when working with and sharing images.

In addition to its image sharing capabilities, ActiveShare also offers some image editing functions, although they are not as extensive as the ones in PhotoDeluxe itself.

ActiveShare software

ActiveShare is provided with PhotoDeluxe and it can also be downloaded from the following site:

- http://www.activeshare.com/

The ActiveShare site can also be accessed through the Adobe site at:

http://www.adobe.com

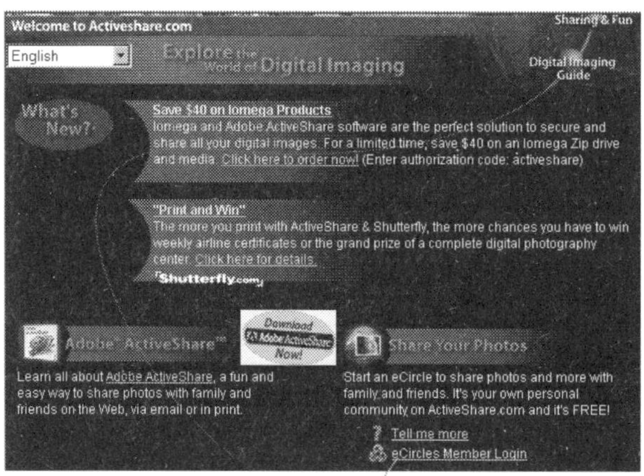

Click here on the ActiveShare Home Page to download the ActiveShare software

At present, there is not a version of ActiveShare available for Mac users.

Creating albums

The ActiveShare interface is very similar to that of PhotoDeluxe, so anyone new to the program will feel at home almost immediately. As well as its Web sharing capabilities, ActiveShare also allows you to store and edit your images. The first step in this process is to create an album where you are going to keep images in ActiveShare:

ActiveShare is an excellent option for creating image albums so that you can view a lot of images quickly. However, for most editing and special effects functions, PhotoDeluxe offers a wider variety.

1 Select Create Album

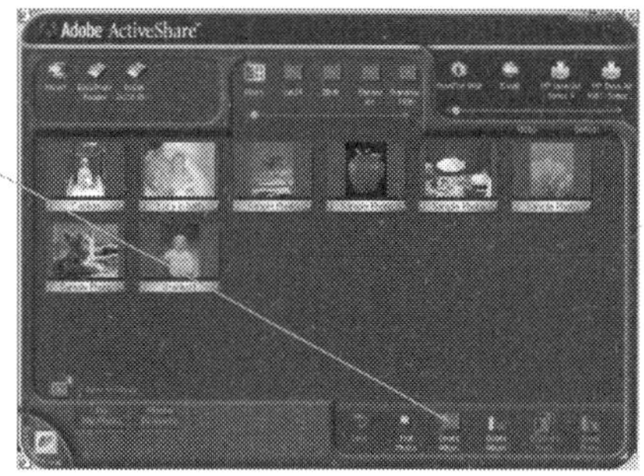

Numerous albums can be created but only one can be opened at any one time. Double-click on an album to open it.

2 Select a name for the album and where you want to store it — on your computer or on a type of removable storage. Select OK

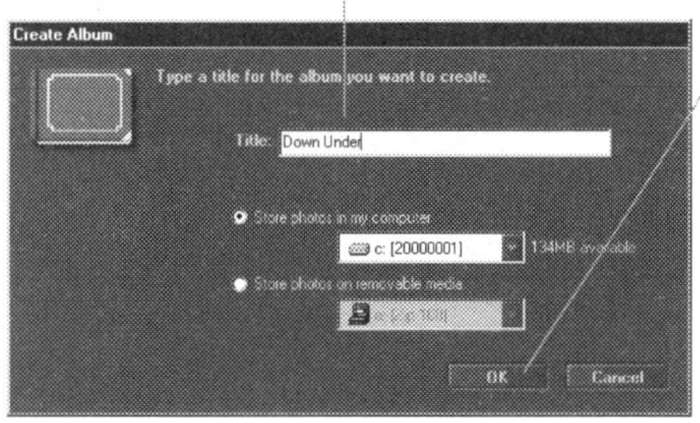

Albums that are created in PhotoDeluxe can be opened directly in PhotoDeluxe, using the My Photos option as the source for opening images.

3 The new album appears here

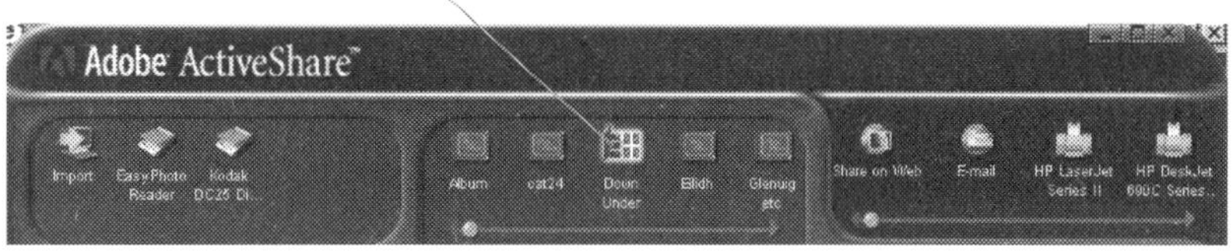

Importing images

Images can be opened in ActiveShare from either the hard drive, a digital camera or a scanner:

1 Double-click on an album to open it

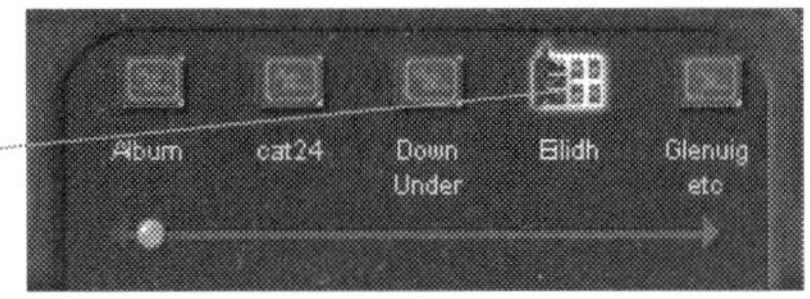

2 Select Import to open an image from the computer's hard drive

It is possible to load more than one image from the hard drive at a time. Hold down Ctrl when you are selecting the images and then click on all of the ones that you want to copy into the open ActiveShare album.

3 Select an image from the Import dialog box and select Open

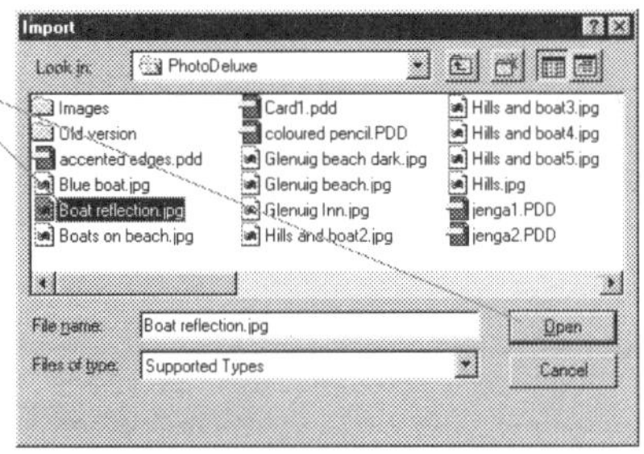

4 To open an image from a digital camera or a scanner, click here to view the available options

5 Select the appropriate device and then double-click on the device to access the images

Editing images

Although ActiveShare does not have the editing power or versatility of PhotoDeluxe, it does offer some basic functions that can be used to enhance images:

1. Open an album and select an image. Select Fix My Photo to access the editing options

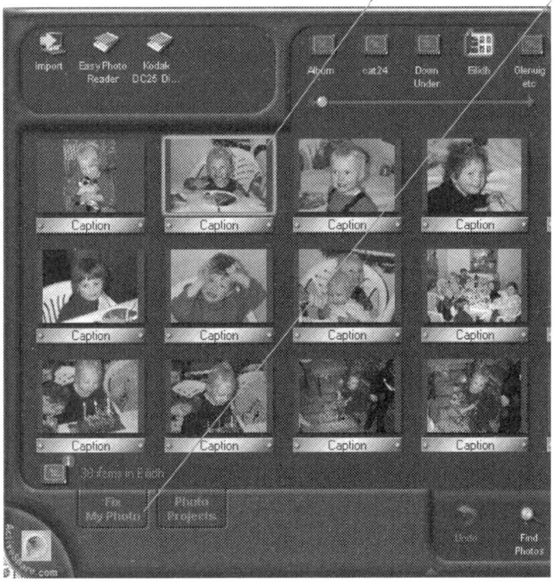

If you select More Tools... from the editing options menu, a window with information about PhotoDeluxe and Photoshop LE appears. If you select the More About PhotoDeluxe or More About Photoshop LE buttons, you will be taken automatically to the relevant pages on the Adobe Website.

2. Do any of the following:
   - Select Instant Fix for all of the colour attributes of the image to be adjusted
   - Select Rotate to change the orientation of an image
   - Select Trim to crop an image
   - Select Remove Red Eye to edit red-eye in an image (see the HOT TIP)

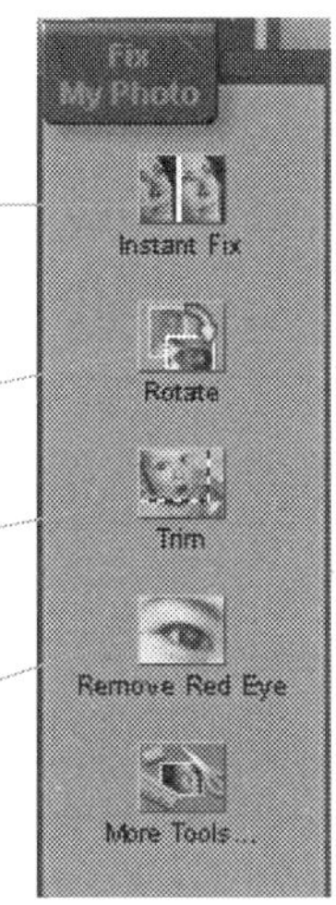

To remove red-eye, size a box around the affected eye and then select the Remove Red Eye button from the Remove Red Eye menu.

Projects

ActiveShare has a small but useful selection of project options so that your images can be put to additional uses:

1. Open an album and select an image. Select Photo Projects

View as Slide Show displays images at their largest possible size to fit the monitor being used. It is therefore an excellent option when viewing images or showing them to other people.

Create WallPaper sets the selected image as your computer's wallpaper. This is done automatically when this option is selected

View as Slide Show enables all of the images in the selected album to be viewed consecutively at full screen size

Add Motion gives the impression of speed in an image, by adding a blurred effect. This can be done from either the left or the right

The Add Motion option should only be used for objects that actually are moving, such as vehicles or people. If it is added to a static object it just looks like it is a blurred image.

Naming and finding images

Images in ActiveShare can be individually named and it is also possible to conduct a search through your albums to find specific images.

Keep image titles short, so you can see the whole of them in the caption box.

Naming images

1 When an image is opened in ActiveShare it is titled Caption

Words that are used in a search for images are known as keywords. These can match up with the same word or words in an image caption and they can also make a match if any of the keywords appear in the details of the source folder from where the image was imported. For instance, if an image came from a folder called Summer Holidays, a search using the keyword Holidays would find this image.

2 Click once on the image to select it and then click on Caption to add your own name for the image

Finding images

1 Select Find Photos

2 In the Find Photos dialog box, enter the search criteria and specify whether you want to search in a specific album or all of your albums. Select Find

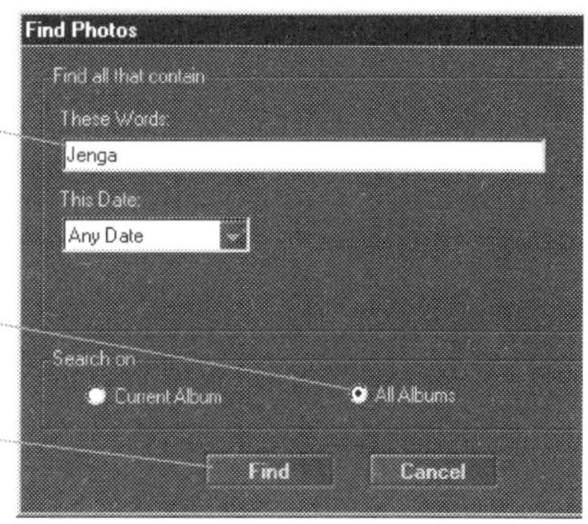

Printing and faxing

Once images have been imported into ActiveShare and edited, they can then be used in a variety of ways. One of the most valuable of these is sharing the images on the Web and this will be dealt with in the next section. However, images can also be used in the following ways by accessing the options here:

Select an option for using images

Printing

ActiveShare may display a number of different printers alongside the printer that is connected to the computer. These options will only work if the relevant printer is connected and the printer drivers installed.

1. Select an image and click here to select a printer

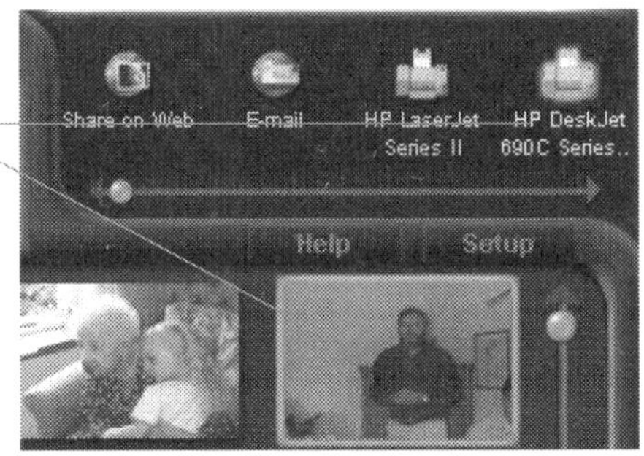

2. Select the required print options from the printer dialog box. Click Optional Settings to go to your printer's normal Print Setup dialog box

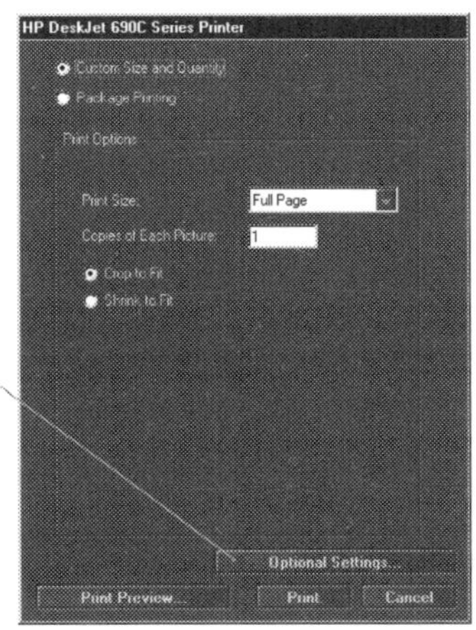

Faxing

If you have the capability for sending faxes from your PC you can do this directly from ActiveShare:

1. Select an image and select a fax printer if one is installed

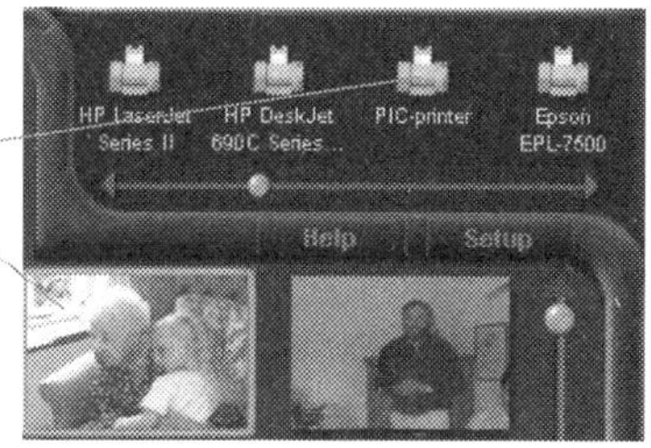

A fax can only be sent from your computer if it has the relevant software installed. This is frequently preloaded on recently produced PCs.

2. Select Optional Settings in the fax printer dialog box

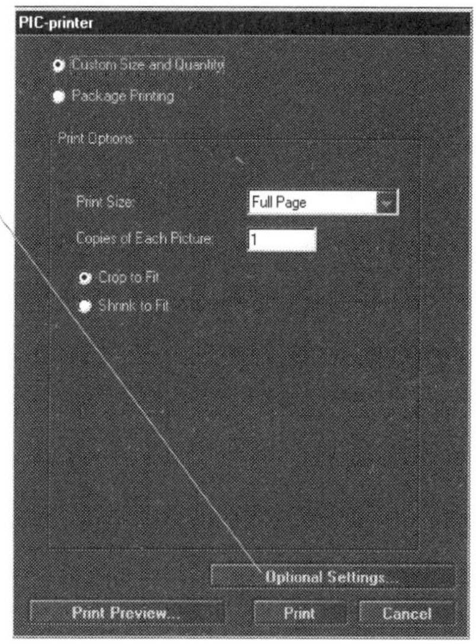

Other uses for images include saving them to a Zip disc and saving a copy to the hard drive.

3. Select the right details for the fax printer and select OK to send the image as a fax

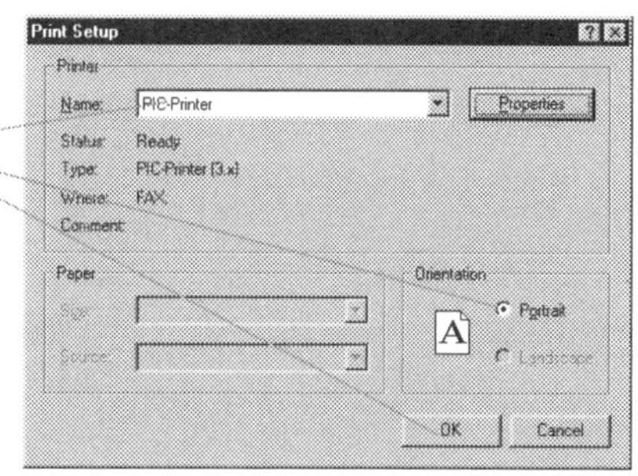

Sharing with ActiveShare

Sharing images is where ActiveShare really comes into its own. By connecting to the ActiveShare Website it is possible to post images on the Web and then designate exactly who is going to have access to view them. This is known as an eCircle. The first step to creating an eCircle is to post an image to the ActiveShare Website. To do this:

It is completely free to create an eCircle and there are no hidden costs to consider, only normal telephone charges while you are connected to the Internet.

1 Select an image and click Share on Web to place it on the Web. This will automatically activate your Internet connection

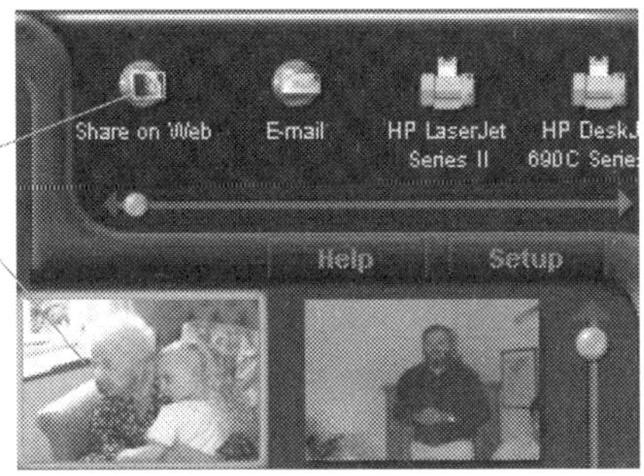

2 In the Login dialog box select Sign Up

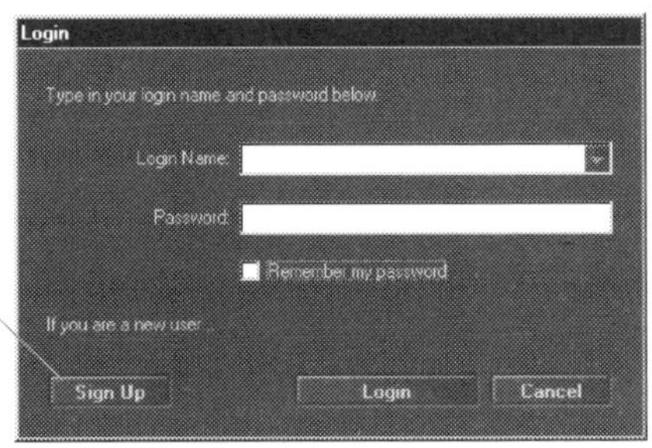

3 Fill in your registration details and then select Next at the bottom of the page

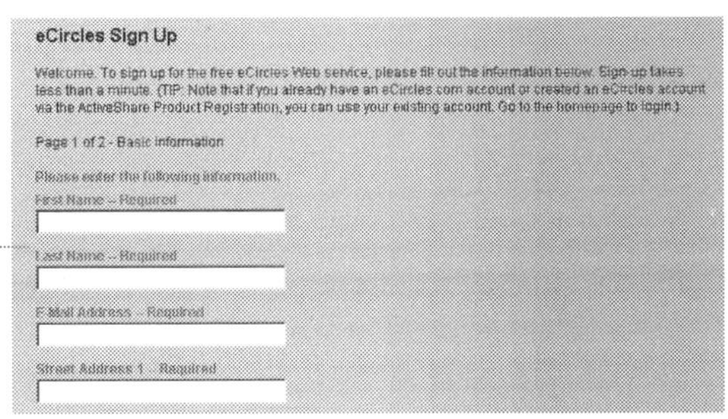

4 Enter a login name and password. Select Sign Up at the end

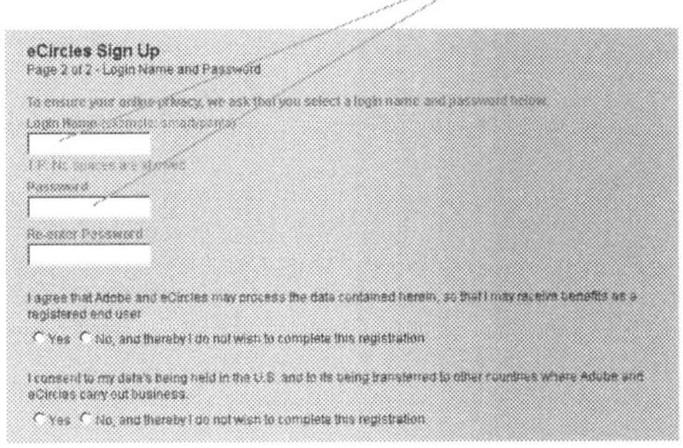

If at any stage during the registration process you enter incorrect information you will be alerted to this and asked to enter something else.

5 If you have completed the registration process correctly the Adobe eCircles window should appear. Close the browser window to return to ActiveShare and Share on Web

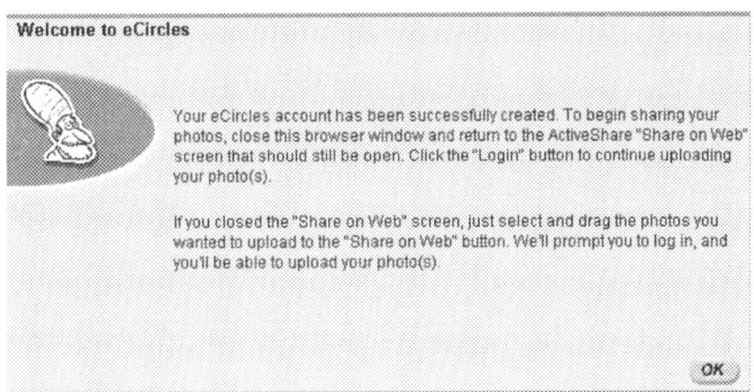

6 Enter your new login name and password and select Login

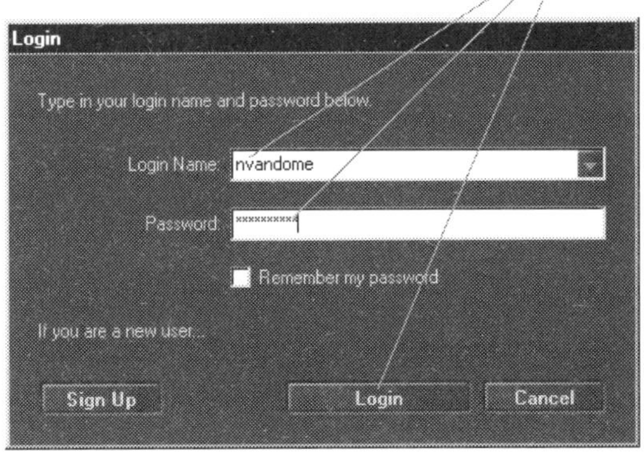

7 Your first eCircle will have been created automatically, for you to upload your images to. Select Continue

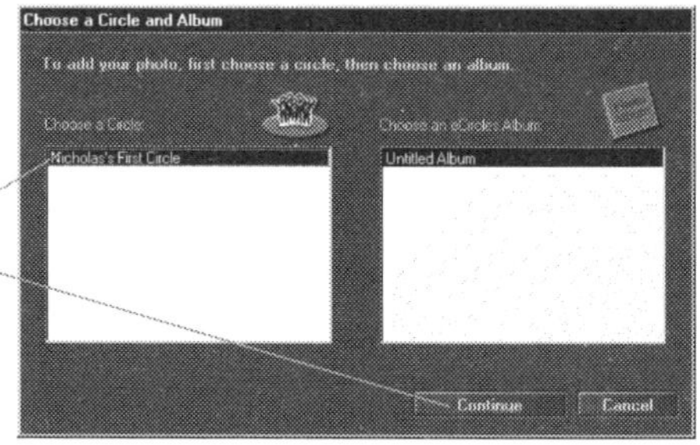

You can create separate albums within each eCircle. Therefore you could have an eCircle called Family and separate albums for each family member. Then, when someone is invited to the eCircle, they will have access to all of the albums.

8 A dialog box will appear, telling you how many images will be uploaded and how long it will take. Select Add Photos Now

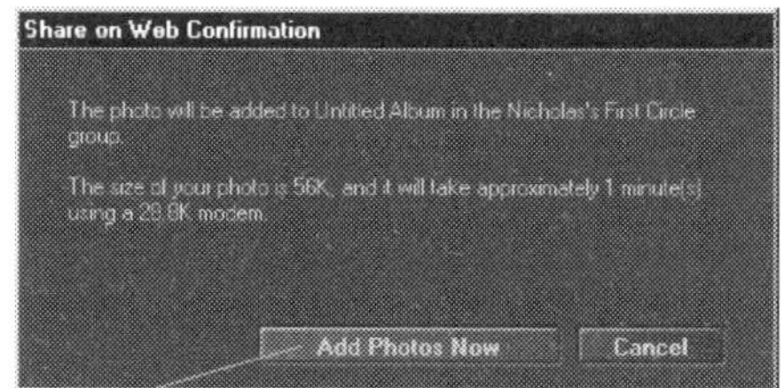

9 If you want to view your images on the eCircle select Yes in the Photo(s) Successfully Added dialog box

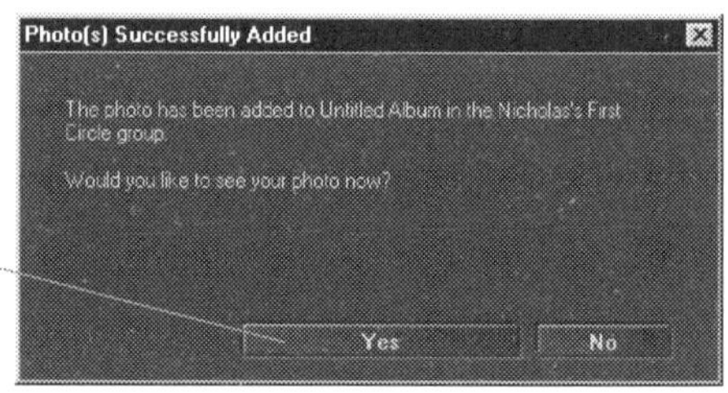

For more information about eCircles, see page 182.

Adding to an eCircle

Once you have registered with ActiveShare and created your first eCircle, you can add more images at any time. The process is similar to adding your first images. To do this:

To select more than one image to share on the Web, hold down Ctrl and select the relevant images by clicking on them. To select a block of images, click on the first one, hold down Shift and then click on the last one. The selected images and all of the ones in between will be selected.

2 Click on Share on Web and connect to the Internet

1 Select a single or multiple images (see the HOT TIP)

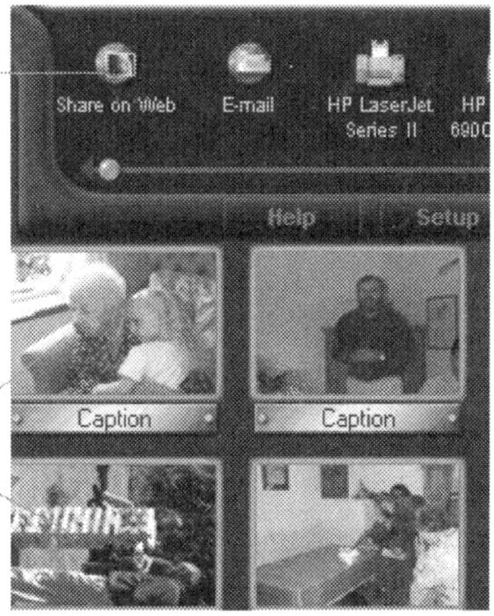

In the ActiveShare Login dialog box, check on the Remember my Password box so that you do not have to enter your login details every time.

3 Enter your ActiveShare login name and password. Select Login

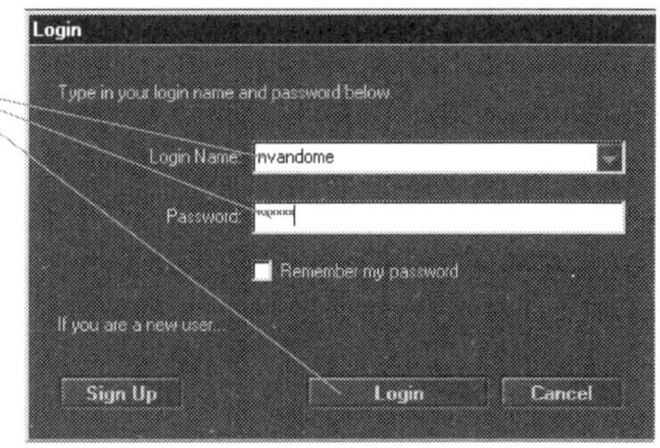

4 Select an eCircle and an Album into which you want to add your images. Select Continue to have them added

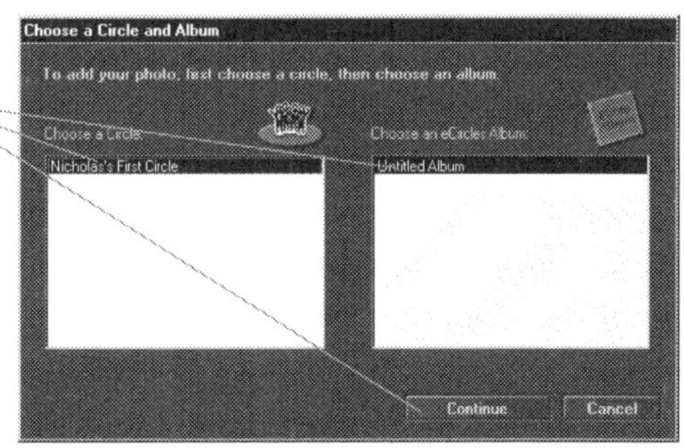

Emailing and other functions

As with PhotoDeluxe it is possible to share images through ActiveShare by emailing them to people. To do this:

2 Click on the Email button

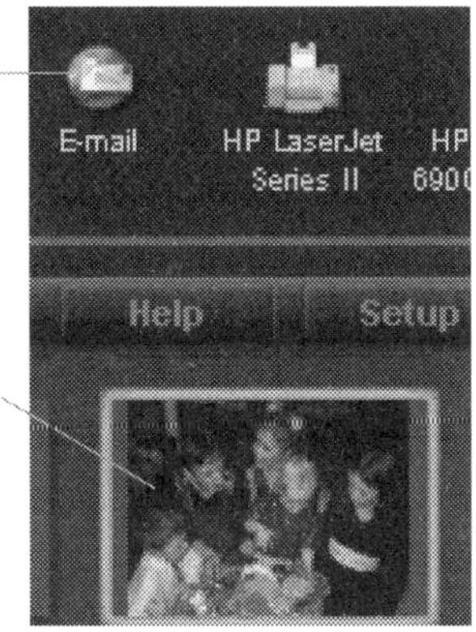

1 Select an image

Images can also be sent by email using the attachment option that is present in most email programs. This is usually denoted by a paperclip icon and this enables you to select an image from your computer and attach it to your text email message.

3 In the Email dialog box enter the details for who the email is from, who it is going to and the message that goes with it. Select Send and the message and the image will be sent to the recipient. If you are not already online then ActiveShare will automatically connect you to the Internet and your email program

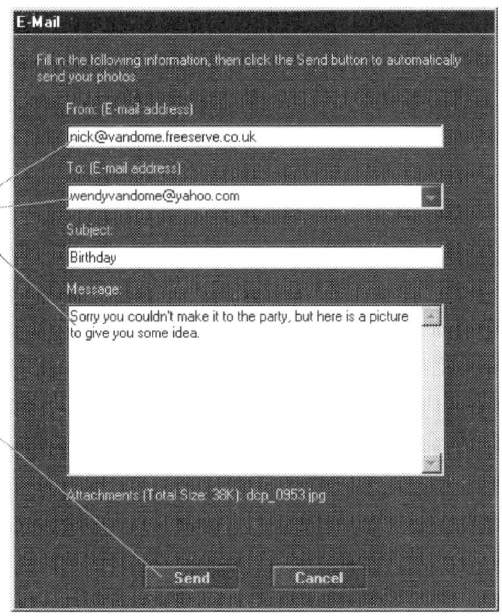

The Email dialog box displays the size of the image, or images, that you are attaching to the email to send. This is a useful way to see how large the overall email will be in view of downloading time.

Send to PhotoDeluxe

The Send to PhotoDeluxe option is a useful one if you want to perform editing tasks that cannot be done in ActiveShare or if you want to use the image in a card or similar projects.

1. Select an image
2. Click on the Send to PhotoDeluxe button to open the image in PhotoDeluxe

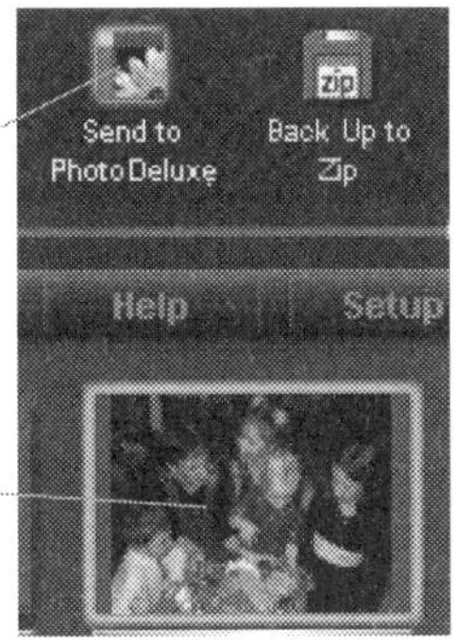

Back Up to Zip

Zip discs are like inflated floppy discs and generally hold either 100 Mb or 250 Mb of data.

1. Select an image and click on the Back Up to Zip button

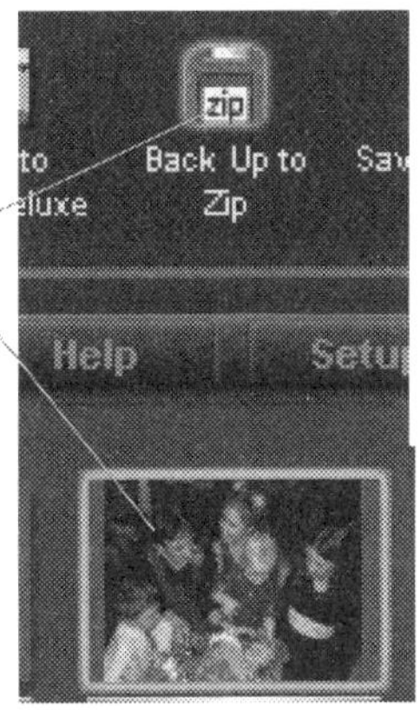

Always back up your images because you never know when your hard drive my have a fatal crash i.e. stop working permanently. If this happens it could cause a lot of distress if you cannot retrieve your images.

2. Insert a Zip disc and select the relevant drive in the Back Up To Zip dialog box. Select Back Up

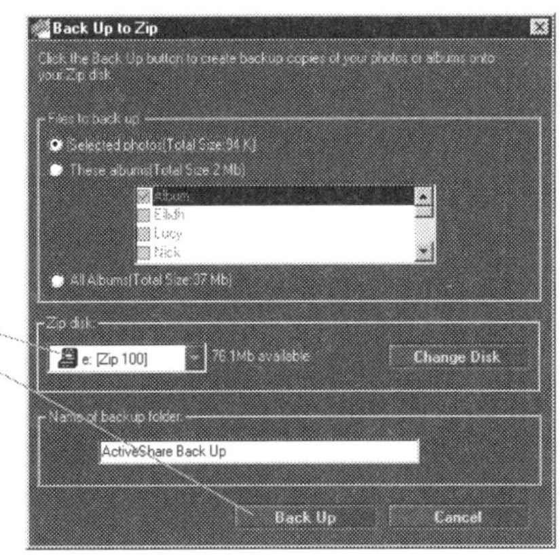

Using eCircles

Once you have registered with ActiveShare and created your first eCircles you can then start working with them.

Opening an eCircle

To open an eCircle:

For quick access to the ActiveShare Website, add it to your Favorites (Internet Explorer browser) or Bookmarks (Navigator browser) list. Then when you want to go there, select Favorites (or Bookmarks) and select ActiveShare from the list that appears.

1. Connect to the Internet and select eCircles Member Login on the ActiveShare home page

2. Enter your Login Name and Password. Select Log In

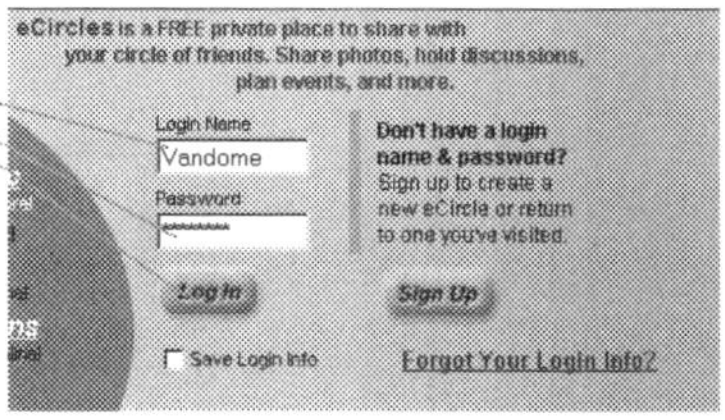

On the ActiveShare home page there are also options for buying reduced-price Zip drives and discs and for getting hardcopy prints of your digital images, using a service called Shutterfly.

3. In the My Circles window, all of your eCircles will be displayed. Click one to access it

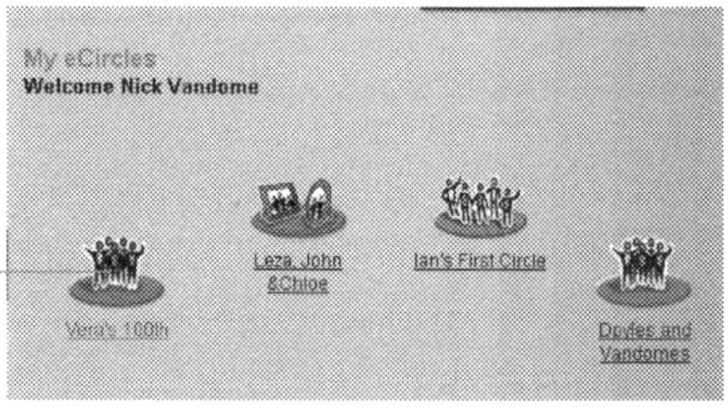

4. Click on Photo Albums to see all of the albums within that eCircle. Then click on the cover of an album to see all of the images which it contains

Inviting more people

The object of creating eCircles is to let other people see the fruits of your digital labour. This can be done by emailing people to invite them to a particular eCircle. The recipient will then receive a message inviting them to the eCircle and a link directly to ActiveShare so that they can register. To invite more people:

1. Open an eCircle but do not access any of its albums

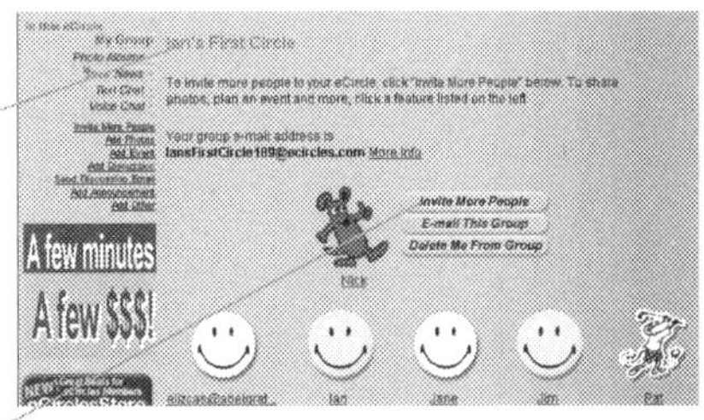

2. Select the Invite More People button

3. Enter the email addresses of the people you want to invite to your eCircle. Use the preset message that the recipients will receive, or write your own

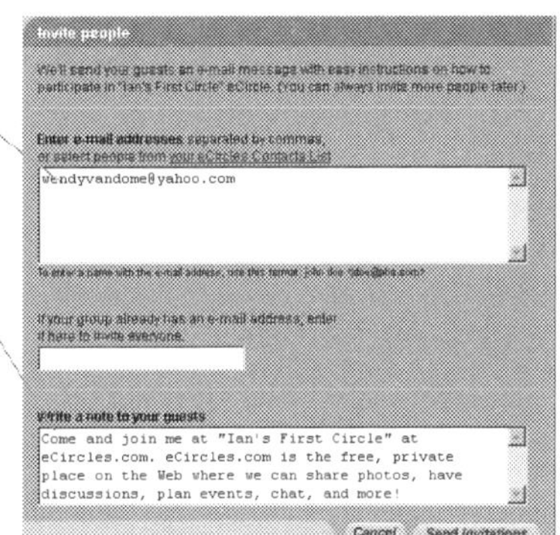

4. Select the Send Invitations button. A dialog box will appear telling you that the invitations have been sent successfully. Select Done

PhotoDeluxe, ActiveShare and eCircles all integrate very closely:

- *PhotoDeluxe is used to edit images and post them onto the Web*
- *ActiveShare is similar, but with a greater emphasis on sharing and creating eCircles*
- *eCircles are for viewing the images and letting other people see them over the Web*

When inviting people to an eCircle, make sure you type their email addresses correctly, otherwise they will not receive the invitation. If you are inviting more than one person, separate the addresses with a comma.

Other people can invite you to view their eCircles too. If you want to remove yourself from a particular eCircle, open it and select the Delete Me From Group button.

Checking activity

If you have several eCircles, with a lot of members in each of them, then there may be a lot of activity with which to keep up. Rather than having to access each album in each eCircle when you want to see what has been happening, ActiveShare offers two ways to keep you up-to-date. The first is by sending you an email whenever there has been any activity in any one of your eCircles. You can specify how often you want this to happen as follows:

1. In the eCircles opening page, select Password & Settings

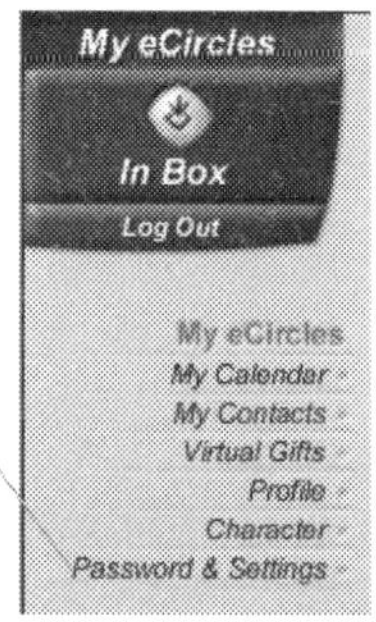

The Password and Setting dialog box can also be used to change your password. Click on the Password link and in the Password dialog box enter your existing password. Then in the box below, enter the new password you want to use. Re-enter this in the next box and click on the Update button. If you forget your password at any time, click on the Forgot Your Login Info? button on the eCircles login page.

2. In the Password & Settings dialog box, click on the E-mail Notification link

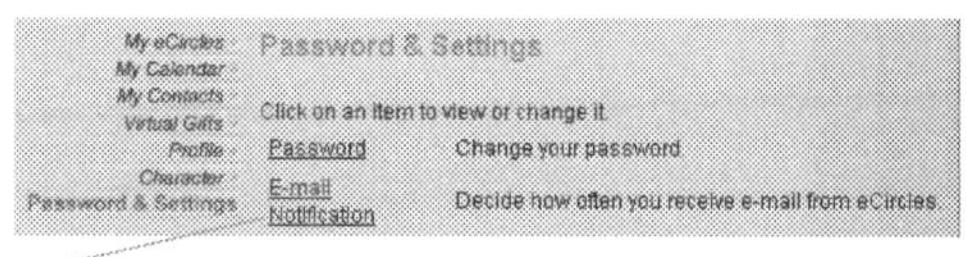

3. Select the details for how often you want to be notified about new activity in your eCircles, whether you want to receive news from eCircles, and other information about your eCircles

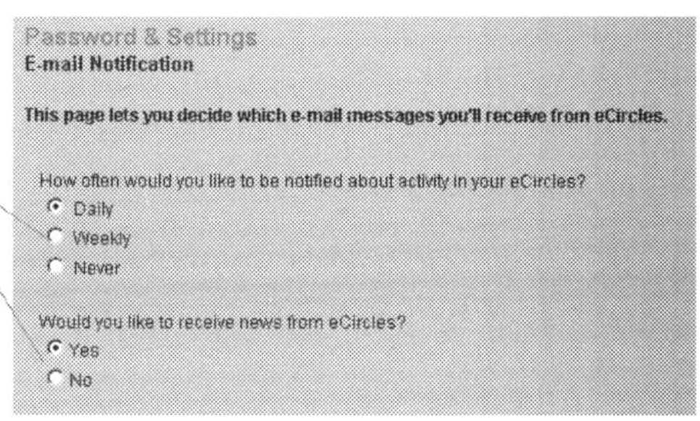

The other way to find out about activity in your eCircles is to look in your In Box. This is similar to an email Inbox and keeps note of everything that happens in your eCircles. The In Box is always available, regardless of which eCircle or album you are viewing.

Viewing the contents of the In Box

DON'T FORGET

It is a good idea to delete items from your In Box once you have accessed them and viewed the new activity. This will make it look less cluttered the next time you look in it. To delete items, either select the Delete All button or check on the box next to an item to select it and then select the Delete Selected button.

1. At any time while you are within eCircles, click on the In Box button, which is located at the top left-hand corner of the program

2. A new window will open, with all of the most recent activity within your eCircles. Click on the relevant item to take you directly to the new activity

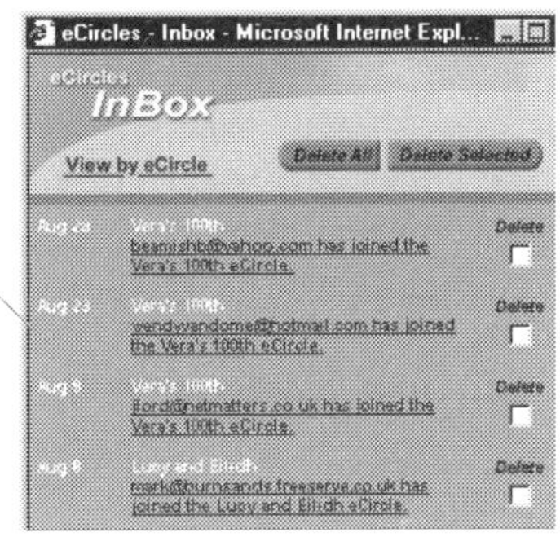

DON'T FORGET

If you want to close down eCircles at any point, select the Log Out button that is underneath the In Box button.

Returning home

If at any point while you are viewing your eCircles and albums you want to return to the page that lists all of your different eCircles, this can be done by clicking on the My eCircles button that is always visible above the In Box button:

Click here at any time to return to your eCircles home page

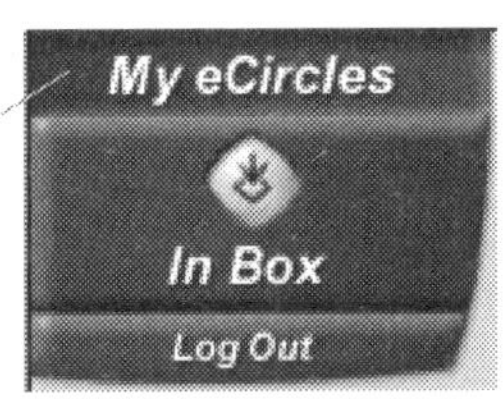

User information

When you create eCircles you can enter details about yourself so that other members can find out a bit more about you. You can add as much or as little information as you like and you can decide what information is available to each of your eCircles. To set your user profile:

You can enter your birthday in the Personal section of the user profile. If you do this, all of the other members of that eCircle will receive a reminder that it is your birthday soon. This is a good way to ensure a few birthday emails or even virtual birthday cards or gifts.

1. From your eCircles home page, click on Profile

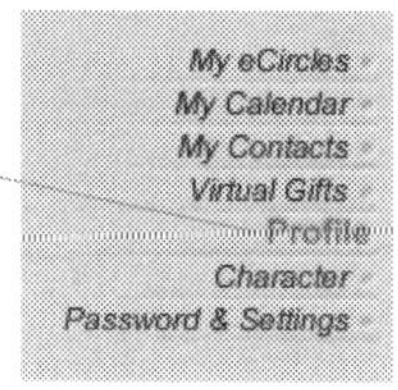

2. Enter the details about yourself that you want the other eCircle members to see. Click on the tabs to enter different types of information

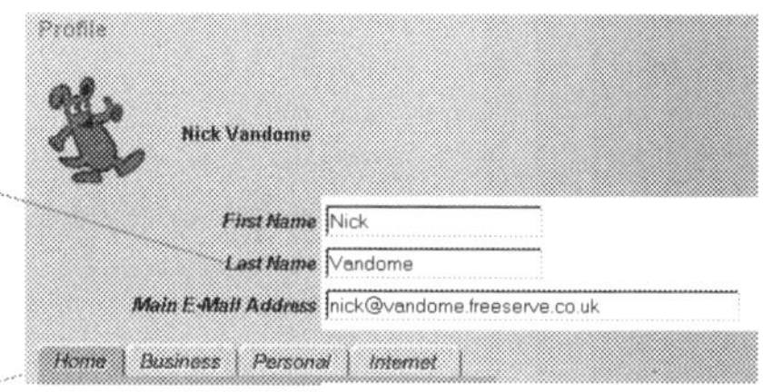

Specifying access to your user details:

Each member of an eCircle can specify a character that is used to depict them. By default this is a smiley face but this can be altered to make it more personal. To do this, select the Character button from the eCircle home page. Then select a category and choose a character that you feel best matches your own. You can change your character to another at any time.

1. In the Password & Settings dialog box, select the Profile Access link

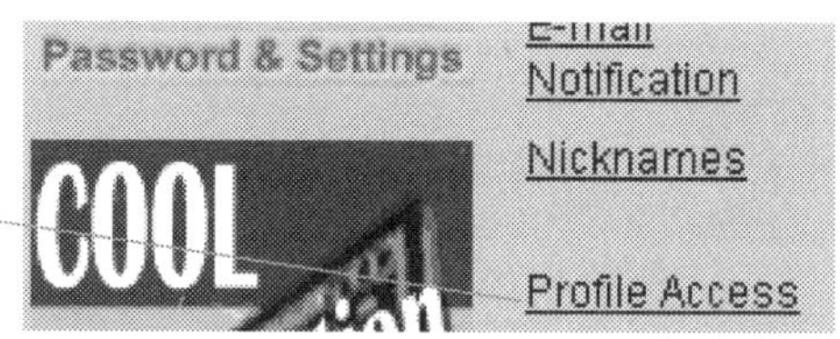

2. Check on the boxes to make that heading of information available to a specified eCircle

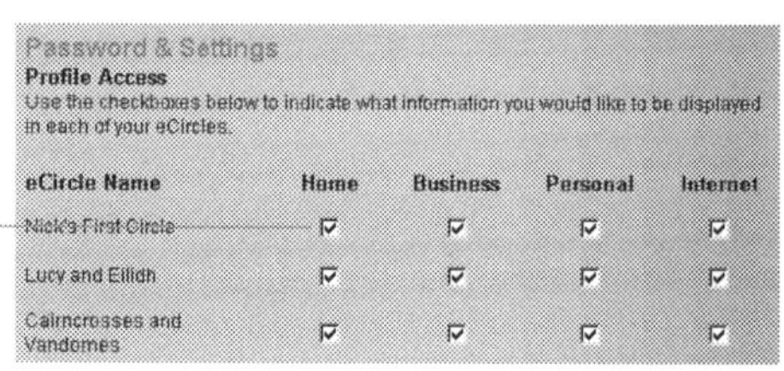

Index

S